Hot Chocolate
for a
Cold Winter Night

Exercises for Relationship Enhancement

Dorothy Becvar
Radford University (Virginia)

Ray Becvar
St. Louis Family Institute

D1364805

LOVE PUBLISHING COMPANY®
Denver, Colorado 80222

Library of Congress Catalog Card Number 94-75176

Copyright © 1994 Love Publishing Company
Printed in the U.S.A.
ISBN 0-89108-233-6

TABLE OF CONTENTS

For Lynne

Preface

The essays and exercises presented in this volume are designed to help couples enhance their relationships and are most appropriate for improving an already satisfactory marriage/relationship. We recommend that both members of the couple read this book together because relationships are bilateral. By this we mean people in a relationship mutually and simultaneously influence each other; influence is never unilateral or one-directional. To incorporate new information or make a decision to change something in your relationship without the knowledge of the other is thus to attempt a unilateral change in something that is bilateral and the result is likely to be confusion and/or resistance, despite your best intentions.

In writing and organizing our material, we included a variety of ideas and activities that have proven useful in our many years of working with couples in premarital and marital/couple therapy and enrichment. However, we were aware of what may be seen as a basic contradiction. On the one hand, we believe that there is no particular way couples *should* be and that what constitutes a "good" marriage/relationship is personal to each couple and to the unique characteristics that each partner brings to the relationship. On the other hand, we believe that successful relationships are firmly grounded in strong, caring, nurturing behaviors, and thus we have focused on ways to facilitate such behaviors.

The tone of the essays and exercises was influenced by a pattern in thinking we have often observed in couples in both therapy and relationship enhancement workshops. This pattern is what Gregory Bateson has described as the clinical bias "that there are good things and there are bad things. The bad things necessarily have causes. This is not so true of good things" (Bateson in Brand, 1974, p. 25.). Thus relationships tend to become problem-saturated and problem-focused. By contrast, a large part of our work involves helping couples focus on the "causes" of the good things that are a part of any relationship. We help them become aware of what each does to create the good things that occur and encourage an increase in the relative frequency of these behaviors. It is our belief that putting something new in forces something else out. This translates into the idea that as the frequency of efforts to produce positive things increases, the number of negative things experienced is reduced.

Another aspect of thinking that couples often present is reflected in what to us is a corollary of Bateson's observation about the clinical bias. In any relationship one can observe as many similarities as differences, and the key to the quality experienced in a relationship is the degree to which the focus is on similarity or on difference. A focus on difference increases the probability that the partners will engage in a high frequency of efforts to change one another, which may also lead to a problem-saturated relationship. To make things worse, the similarities between the two people in the relationship often get lost when all the attention is focused on difference and reciprocal efforts to reduce difference. Many end up being similar only in their efforts to change each other.

We therefore value and would hope to influence you to focus on and increase the frequency of the positive things that happen in your relationship. We encourage you to become aware that each of you is a "cause" of such good things. And we believe that as you make conscious efforts to make good things happen in your relationship, and as you focus more on similarities, the frequency of bad things and reciprocal attempts to eliminate differences will be reduced.

There are other values that will become apparent to you as you read through the essays and exercises. For example, while we believe that a good relationship is one in which the two people involved can grow and develop, how that looks will be different for each couple. Similarly, we believe that a good relationship is one in which each person has the freedom to be different and is able to accommodate the difference of the other. For if we insist that the other be the way we want that person to be, we probably will create not only a mess but also a whole lot of pain.

Another stance we value is, "If it ain't broke, don't fix it." If you already have a relationship with which you are comfortable, don't try to change it. Rather, relax and enjoy it. Indeed, we believe that Utopian notions about relationships may do more harm than good by posing ideals that are unrealistic and unattainable. On the other hand, since we believe that we all are able to learn and grow until the day we die, it is not necessarily harmful to be open to new ideas that may add a bit of zest or spark creativity in our relationships. The important point is that we pick and choose carefully and that we be realistic in our expectations. No person or marriage/relationship is perfect, or even okay, 100 percent of the time. So if your relationship is satisfactory 75 percent of the time, we think you are doing great.

A most important value for us is respect for each couple's right to decide what fits for them and what does not fit. Our way is not *the* way. Generic models are only generally useful and may or may not fit the unique emotional system that is each relationship. Indeed, your relationship with your partner and every other relationship in your life is a unique emotional system.

As you read the essays and experience the exercises, we encourage you to reflect, to prioritize, and to examine the kind of energy you are now expending in your marriage/relationship. And as you read these, or any other ideas on improving your relationship, we encourage you to dismiss that which does not fit while accepting those which do. While we believe that a happy relationship is one in which its members make happy things happen, what constitutes a "happy thing" is unique to the members of that relationship.

Enjoy!

Dorothy S. Becvar
Raphael J. Becvar

Chapter 1

Thinking About Relationships

There are many ways to think about the relationships in our lives. And we seem to spend a great deal of our time thinking about them, for much of both our satisfaction and our dissatisfaction in living is closely tied to the quality of our relationships. Salvador Minuchin (1984) provides the following comment, which we find useful in thinking about relationships. It also may be useful to you. He writes:

> All we know for sure is that each scenario is an experiment in living. Thus, by definition, it will be carried out in an unstable field, full of visible and hidden traps. The only certainty is that there will be errors and, because of them, conflict, solutions, and growth. (p. 45)

Each new setting that we experience and each new relationship in our lives is an experiment and challenges us to find a way to be and do what feels most appropriate to that scenario. A dictionary definition of scenario is, "an outline or synopsis of a play, the book of an opera, etc., showing the scenes and the entrances and exits of the actors." If we use the scenario, or theater, analogy to think about our relationships, we could say that each member has a different script and outline for the common drama of the relationship and how it should be played. A relationship can thus be described as two people trying to forge a coordinated performance while using two different scripts. Each plays his/her part in the manner that seems most appropriate to him/her and tries to elicit from the other behaviors complementary to one's own desired role. If the other does not play the role in a way that fits the envisioned scene, attempts are made to reshape the role of the other. So, while each person in a relationship is an actor, each is also a director, attempting to choreograph the movement, delivery, and development of the scene in the unfolding drama that is the relationship.

Sometimes the two separate scripts are quite naturally complementary and the relationship drama seems to flow effortlessly and smoothly as each member plays his/her role in a way that closely approximates the scenario envisioned by the other. At other times the two separate scripts are quite different and the relationship drama evolves into one in which both actors become directors engaging in reciprocal attempts to get the other to play opposite him/her in ways that fit different visions.

No two scripts in any relationship are identical, but if the scripts fit well together, the members will spend more time acting and less time directing than if their scripts are different. Indeed, one measure of the quality of a relationship is the relative amount of time the actors spend in the acting versus the directing roles. Practically speaking, in a less than satisfactory relationship there is likely to be a higher frequency of talking about the behaviors and attitudes of the members and about the relationship.

While, as noted above, no two scripts are ever identical, there probably are as many similarities between them as there are differences. Our experience suggests that a focus on differences evokes director roles while a focus on similarities evokes actor roles, thus facilitating a more positive drama. Further, according to Minuchin (1984):

> Answers are born in the way we pose questions. When we look seriously at people interacting with each other, measuring their interactions and applying prevalent norms to the interpretation of our findings, our results can elicit either concern or laughter. Looking at life, as I do, as sets of unfilled promises, I think that on the whole I prefer laughter.

Ideally, if one member's script is A and the other's is B, a C script accommodating both of the actors will evolve. There will be an acceptance of differences and a recognition that a perfect fit is not possible. And the C script will include fun and laughter.

We ask you now to experiment with the first formal exercise that is a part of the scenario of this book. While trying it we ask you to use the script for relationships described above to think about the relationships in your life.

Exercise 1

Find a time when you can each be alone. You will need a notebook and a pen or pencil to record your thoughts. Select three different relationships that are important to you. We suggest that these relationships involve people in different contexts. You might select your relationship with your spouse or significant other; your parents; your children; a friend; a colleague at work. Think about the first relationship you have chosen. Become consciously aware of the script and scenario that you have for this relationship and how it should be played. Do this in great detail. Become aware of and record the frequency of time you spend "acting" and the amount of time you move up to the level of "director" and try to choreograph this relationship. Now do the same thing for the other two relationships you have selected, using a separate page for each.

Exercise 2

With each of the relationships you identified in Exercise 1, we ask that you focus on and try to envision the script and scenario that the other person has for this relationship and how it should be played. As much as you can, through your vision of the other person's actions, record the frequency of time the other spends "acting" and the amount of time he or she moves up to the level of "director" and tries to choreograph this relationship.

While we believe it is important that both of you do the above exercises, we suggest that you not discuss your experiences with each other or anyone else. Allow yourselves to reflect and come to your own personal conclusions. The significance lies in this process of reflection for each of you.

Chapter 2

Before the Beginning

A question we would like to ask you, as we do whenever we meet with a couple for the first time, is "How did you meet?" Other questions we might ask are: "What was your first impression of your husband/wife/partner?" "Who initiated the first date?" "What did you like/love about the other that influenced you to contemplate marriage or a committed relationship?" These questions are designed to take you back before the beginning, when you were first establishing your relationship. As time goes by the answers to such questions become more and more important for they act as reminders of how you each used to be with each other during a very special period in your lives. Indeed, the answers may provide a stimulus for reexperiencing the excitement of your initial encounter and courtship.

You might argue that those days are long gone and that you do not feel particularly hopeful that they will ever return. You might also say that too much time has passed and that the illusions of courtship have given way to the reality of day-to-day living. Certainly many people experience the changes in their relationship over time in this way. Indeed, it is a prevailing story about marriage in our culture that, if believed, becomes a self-fulfilling prophecy and thus reality. But this story is true only if you believe it to be true. Another story that is equally plausible is that the excitement of courtship evolves into mundane reality because couples stop doing, or do far less often, those things that occurred on a spontaneous and impromptu basis before getting married and/or "settling down." In effect, spouses/partners cease or greatly reduce courtship behavior and life thus becomes routine at best and dull or boring at worse.

A marriage or committed relationship is a relationship of choice. If you would like your partner to continue to choose to be married/committed to you, rather than just reconciled to being in the relationship, courtship is an essential ingredient. Indeed, courtship is forever.

Now we are going to invite you to go back to the time when you first met each other, to the initial courtship period of your relationship. As described above, this journey into the past, into the personal history of your relationship, is very important. There are some lessons to be learned from your history, lessons that can enhance your relationship today and in the days that follow.

Exercise 1

Find a place where you can be alone and undisturbed for about an hour. We suggest you sit facing each other and that you make sure the TV is turned off and the phone is off the hook.

Close your eyes and think back to when you first met each other. Get a real picture of the event in your mind's eye. Recall the place, the time, the circumstances, the sounds, the smells, what each of you were wearing. Recall your first impressions of each other. Recall what you felt, said, did. Let yourself be there once again.

Okay, now take a few minutes to share your recollections with each other. Remember, they may be somewhat different, for each of you had a different vantage point, and one may have an eye for more detail than the other. Just reflect, recall, and recount.

There may have been some embarrassment as you recalled and shared your recollections. It may or may not have been "love at first sight." Nevertheless, this was the beginning of your relationship.

Exercise 2

Think back to the period of your courtship, that important time when you were getting to know each other better. Think of the things you did together.

These may have been the times when you were the most open with each other. These were the times when you probably did the small but significant little courtesies that communicated, louder than any words, your affection for one another. Recall them. Close your eyes and let your mind drift back to those days and nights with each other. You were different people then, full of the beautiful dreams and hopes of what your life together would be like. Allow yourself to be there. This may take several minutes. (You also may find yourself replaying this period tomorrow, next week, or next month.)

Share your recollections with each other. Again, what each of you recalls may be very different for each of you has a different perspective.

It was out of this period of courtship that you provided each other with information about yourselves. You probably made a conscious effort to put your best foot forward. You wanted to be loved and to love. And during this time you did things that were loving, and you demonstrated that you knew how to love by doing loving things.

But a strange and almost universal thing happens as a couple goes down the aisle away from the altar. The very fact of making a commitment and publicly affirming that commitment to each other seems to transform the relationship. It is as though you feel you can now relax, let your hair down, and be yourself. So there are surprises as you spend more and more time together and your lives become intricately intertwined. There are also necessary adaptations as you each become aware of your partner's idiosyncrasies. This is normal. This is expected. Unfortunately, what is not expected and what is more important is that the small courtesies and considerations you gave each other during the courtship soon begin to drop off. Thus, not only do you have to adapt to behaviors of your partner about which you had no previous knowledge, but you have a drop in frequency of the little special things you had come to expect.

Those courtesies and thoughtful little things you did in your courtship days were important then and are important today. Perhaps you still do these things. Often, however, they are post-crisis activities or a part of formal holidays like birthdays, Christmas, or Valentine's day. While acknowledging these special occasions is significant, it is not sufficient. The little thoughtful things done just because, as you did in the days of courtship, are the best way we know to "work at" making your marriage/relationship successful.

Making happy things happen or being thoughtful in your relationship energizes, revitalizes, and somehow makes the inevitable crises and process of adjustment seem more bearable, more hopeful. Crises drain energy reserves. We know of no better way to replenish these energy reserves than to be proactive in your relationship. And this means leaving nothing to chance or circumstance.

Routine, daily, mundane activities characterize most couples' lives together. There are things that must be done: children to feed, clothes to wash, houses to clean, grass to mow, etc. Such activities cannot be neglected. Likewise, to make your marriage/relationship successful, there are certain things that need to be done. We believe you should *consciously and conscientiously plot to make happy things happen.* Times together must be scheduled and adhered to just as rigidly as you adhere to your household and work schedule.

Each of you already knows how to do many special, small things for the other. You did them in courtship. You do them from time to time in your relationship today. We suggest that you examine yourself and what you do in your relationship that says "I love you" more than the words can begin to express. This may seem like a challenge, but we suspect it will be surprisingly easy and fun.

Exercise 3

As you sit facing each other, you should be touching in some way. Look each other in the eyes. Look deep. See the person you fell in love with. Think now about those things you can do to make this important person in your life feel happier, move loved, and more cared about; things, which if you do them, will also help you feel better about yourself. Do not share your thoughts!

Make no public commitment to your spouse/partner or others about what you might do more of, less of, or differently. No resolutions. The commitment you make is to yourself. It depends solely on your own sense of integrity and your personal desire to make your spouse/partner, yourself, and your relationship happy.

Chapter 3

On Change and Changing

People who are dissatisfied with their lives and relationships often flip around the idea of change and changing pretty casually. However, as you can probably attest, it isn't that easy, it's hard to maintain, it involves more than you, and it always also involves you. In this essay we hope to provide you with a realistic perspective on the process of change and changing, an important part of our work with individuals, couples, and families. In order to develop this perspective we present two different models.

I. *The willpower, work-ethic model.* This is the model of change that is most common in our culture. It is the "you can if you want to" or the "little engine that could" model.

The exercises below give you an experience in this model. We ask that you do Exercise 1 before you read the instructions for Exercise 2. (This way you will feel a difference that we want you to experience, and experience is worth 10,000 words.)

Exercise 1

Get a pencil and a sheet of paper. Write your name three times. Do this very quickly. When you have finished, continue with Exercise 2.

Exercise 2

Write your name three times once again. Only this time do it with your opposite hand.

You probably had a reaction like "Oh, no!" when you read the instructions in Exercise 2. So let's focus for a minute on your experience as you wrote your name with your opposite hand. Very possibly you felt uncomfortable, not sure how to grasp the pencil, conspicuous, foolish, and/or unnatural. You probably had to think about how to form the letters. Exercise 2 probably was quite different than Exercise 1, where writing your name was a simple task. In Exercise 2 you were doing a new behavior, beginning a new habit. It is possible, however, that when you wrote your name with your opposite hand for the third time, you did so with greater facility and less discomfort than on your initial attempt. Thus, the assumption of the willpower, work-ethic model is that practice makes perfect and that you can change by your own effort. You can top it off by rewarding yourself or the other person when you or they have been successful in doing the new behavior. This model makes sense for some changes, some of the time.

It is our experience, and an assumption of family systems theory, that behavior change in ongoing relationships, such as a marriage/relationship or family, is a bit more complicated. The work-ethic model makes sense for changes in which the change does not directly affect other people. When the behavior change affects others, like your spouse/partner or children, we find it useful to think differently about change and changing. So now we move to a different model.

II. *The context-relative, you-can't-do-just-one-thing model.* This model suggests that we are not autonomous. Everything we do affects others. To change yourself and to be different in a relationship is to influence the other person. You cannot do just one thing. You cannot change just you. Also, you cannot change others while you stay the same. If a person changes, there is a necessary effect on other people. And other people won't always like the "new" you. This does not mean they are perverse or unsympathetic about what you are trying to be. It suggests that you are different and they don't know who they are and what to do with you the way you are with them and with what you are doing. Their initial response may be to try to change you back to the way you were so that they can know who they are, who you are, and what to do with who you are with them.

Perhaps a couple of examples will help to illustrate the context-relative model. By our behavior we are defining ourselves as teacher and suggesting that you take the role of student. By your behavior you are defining yourself as student and suggesting that we take the role of teacher. One can depict the relationship of the complementary roles of teacher and student as follows:

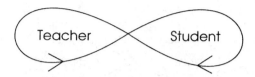

We can maintain the teacher-student relationship only as long as we each continue to behave in a way that is a logical complement to the other. If you cease to behave as a student complementing our behavior as teacher, we would need to maintain our behavior as teacher on our own energy. We would be talking to ourselves, in which case the behavior would wane. Similarly, if we ceased to behave as teacher, you would have to maintain your role as student on your own energy. For another example, imagine yourself telling jokes to an audience that does not laugh. After a few abortive attempts to get them to laugh, it is highly likely that you would soon cease the effort.

When a couple comes in for counseling we thus see their complaints as reciprocal and balanced. He says, "She nags," to which she responds, "He withdraws." Viewed through our eyes, we see their pattern as follows:

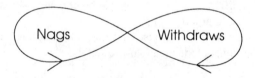

Using the same perspective as we did with the teacher-student relationship, nagging behavior makes sense and thus maintains itself only when complemented with withdrawing behavior, and withdrawing behavior makes sense and thus maintains itself only when complemented with nagging behavior. Each seeks to have the other do behavior other than nagging and withdrawing, and both wind up getting exactly what they don't want.

Change is possible for this couple, but only if each member begins to see that his/her own behavior is a part of the problem. Neither can get what she/he wants if she/he continues to behave in ways that logically complement what is not desired. Thus, it is not that what they want is unattainable; it is just not attainable given what they are doing. A part of our goal, therefore, is to have them understand at some level that for each to get what she/he wants, each has to do a behavior that logically complements the behavior desired from the other.

Thus,

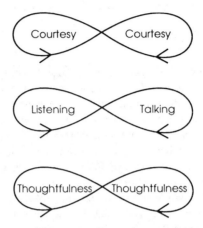

You can't do just one thing. And if you would have others be different with you, the strategy is not to try to change them, but to change yourself so that with you they may be different. Trying to change others while you attempt to stay the same is doomed to failure.

Let's conclude with an exercise that may illustrate the context-relative, you-can't-do-one-thing model in a real-life setting.

Exercise 3

Think of a particular, predictable pattern in your relationship. In order to find something on which to focus, perhaps you may want to visualize a normal day in the life that you share with your spouse/partner. Once you have selected a pattern, decide how you may alter your usual behavior with him or her and then give it a try. However, don't be surprised if your spouse/partner is confused and tries to get the relationship back to the familiar, the predictable, the understandable. Remember, change is both easy and hard. But it can be fun. And it sure helps if both of you see your part in the transactions between you and each takes responsibility for changing his/her part of your interactions.

Chapter 4

"Working At It"

We now offer you a moment of meditation on your life in general and on your marriage/relationship in particular. One of the things that makes human beings unique and, as far as we know, separates us from other organisms is the ability to consciously reflect on experiences and on the purpose and meaning of life. This includes, of course, the ability to reflect on our relationships.

An often-stated cliche, relative to relationships as well as to many other aspects of life is, "You have to work at it." This is consistent with the work ethic into which we were socialized as children and which many of us still use as a measure of whether or not our lives are meaningful. It is not surprising that even our "vacations" may take the form of "working at it"—driving too many miles, in too short a time, to do too many things, and then driving too many miles to get home, to work hard at catching up on the too many things that we didn't do when we were "on vacation." The pace of living seems to be increasing in our society and often we find ourselves running just to keep up with that pace. Somehow, we never seem to get "caught up." And we probably never will. But we keep trying anyway because that's what we're "supposed to do."

Perhaps you have noticed that the busier you are, and the more things you have to do, the more impatient you tend to be with others in your life, and they (rushed and busy in their own ways) are more impatient with you. Unfortunately, this impatience, as reflected in flashes of anger and short, terse responses, tends to occur in the most important relationships—those between spouses/partners and with other family members.

In our work with couples and families we have noticed that some people try to solve their relationship problems in the same way they live their lives, i.e., "working at it" quickly and impatiently, wanting answers and solutions now. We find that sometimes we can help them by encouraging them to slow down and get some distance from themselves and their relationship and, by this distance, to achieve a different view. We illustrate this shift in point of view as follows:

1. Take a moment to recall your experience of the world while sitting in your car with your children in a traffic jam on a hot day.

2. Now take a moment to think about the perspective you have of the world while flying in an airplane at 30,000 feet or sitting quietly in your favorite place.

Sometimes the best way to work at solving problems and building relationships is to not work at solving problems and making the relationship better. Sometimes we just need a period of time to reflect, to think about what it is all about, and to examine and decide which things are really important and should be taken seriously and which things are really only trivial pursuits in the larger scheme of life.

Perhaps you have a memory of times past, or have heard about times past, when there existed the gentle art of porch-sittin', or sittin' and whittlin', and sittin' and knittin'. Perhaps you have paused in your day and watched a baby sleeping or noticed an older person watching the world go by from a favorite park bench. Perhaps you looked into your child's room, which was an absolute mess, paused before you admonished him or her, chuckled, and said "Oh, what the heck!" and quietly closed the door. There are many opportunities each day for these simple pauses, these respites from our routines. But how often do we take advantage of such opportunities?

Sometimes the pauses take another form. In many marriages/relationships there seems to be one spouse who maintains a faster pace, while the other is more laid back. If you are the one who maintains the faster pace, you might just join your spouse/partner and "lay back" together. Or sometimes you might need to "pause to refresh" by yourself. This can be done by arising before the rest of the family gets going. It may be when the kids and your spouse/partner are down for the night and you can sit back in the silence and reflect:

1. Consider yourself: What did you do today that you were pleased at having done? What did you not do today, could have done differently, more of, or less of, in your relationship with your spouse/partner and other members of your family?

2. What things did others do that perhaps hooked an anger response in you that were just not worth the hassle? Did his/her being ten minutes late really make a difference? What's the big deal about forgetting to put away the toothpaste?

3. What things did you do to enjoy yourself today? To enjoy your spouse/partner? Your children?

4. What silly things or happenings occurred today that you might have laughed at, but missed because you were too harried to notice?

5. You might just take time to listen to the sound of silence, to feel the pace of your breathing, to feel the magic workings of your body and to relax, and symbolically do some sittin' and whittlin' or sittin' and knittin.'

Chapter 5

Memories...

One of our goals for you is that you gain a different perspective on your relationship. And one way we try to facilitate this process is by helping you to understand the roots of your relationship and its history. If you read and did the exercises in "Before the Beginning," you have already had one experience in this area. Similarly, memories, especially in the form of pictures or mementos, can help you to recapture the special moments in your life together. They may also encourage you to think differently about where you wish to go from here. It is in this spirit that we invite you to enjoy the following exercises. The first is designed for each of you to do alone. The second is to be done together.

Exercise 1

Each of you take some time to dig out old pictures, slides, movies, scrapbooks, ticket stubs, programs, letters, or whatever you have collected that provides a lasting record of shared events from the earliest days up to the present. After you have completed your individual searches, gather your goodies in a separate box and reflect on what each picture or item means to you without sharing your thoughts with your partner.

Exercise 2

Plan some blocks of time when the two of you can be alone together. We suggest you allow at least two hours and mark the date and time agreed upon on your calendars. Be aware that several such "dates" may be required to cover the territory. This time is to be your private time together and we recommend that it follow a leisurely pace.

At the appointed time, bring yourselves and your favorite beverage and/or food to your memory-sharing place. (Remember to make sure that you will not be disturbed by phones, children, or other uninvited guests.) Now take turns showing each other selections from your boxes. Pull out each item at random and take some time to relive the moments it captures. Perhaps you will be reminded of an event, time, or person you haven't thought about in years. Perhaps you will become aware of the special meanings each of you attributed to these events or times or persons.

After completing this activity, you may choose to share some of your memories with your children. Children are generally curious about their parents and their parents' relationship. The experience of sharing your memories may give them a different perspective on both of you. They may even find that you are real people after all! On the other hand, some of the memories are yours alone. These should be kept private.

While you may have previously done the activities described above, we believe they bear repeating from time to time. And in the days that follow, we invite you to continue your reflections and to take cues from the past about the way you might be in the future.

Chapter 6

Love Is...

The topic of this essay is love. It is a topic with probably as many meanings as there are people in love. The experience of love is, very often, the measure of the quality of a relationship. Attempts to describe love have been made by philosophers, scientists, and poets. However, it is very difficult to define except in very general ways. On a personal level, it is something, "We just know."

Interestingly, "love" as the reason for marrying is a very recent phenomenon. According to the history of most cultures, marriages typically were arranged by the parents. In such arrangements romantic love was not considered important. Liaisons were made for economic and political reasons and for carrying on traditions, and if love happened, it generally was after the fact.

Erich Fromm describes several kinds of love. He also describes what to him are the four basic ingredients to any intimate relationship: care, responsibility, respect, and knowledge. While many other theories are available, we are most concerned with helping you make your love for each other live in your relationship in very tangible ways.

Lynn Scoresby made the following observation:

Since love is the word symbol we are accustomed to using in explaining great varieties of marital events, if actual feelings of love are not determinant of happy marriages, then mutual agreement about what love means is. Love is, after all, the most often given reason for getting married, and loss of love is the most often given reason for dissolving a marriage. (p. 186)

What Scoresby is suggesting is that couples need to agree on what love is to them and what each considers loving acts to be. When they can act on this agreement, then their chances of maintaining love in their relationship are greater. Scoresby suggests further that one must be able to receive love if a relationship is to remain loving. As you accept your partner's love, you affirm him/her as an accepted and valued part of your life.

Drawing on Scoresby's observations, we have several challenges for you. The first is to help you agree upon what each of you defines as loving acts. Next, we invite you to act on this agreement. Finally, we attempt to help you to receive and acknowledge the loving acts of your partner.

Exercise 1

This exercise is a personal challenge for each of you, and you are to do it separately. Each of you will need a tablet or sheet of paper and a pencil. Each of you is to make a list of those things that you presently do, or might do, that your spouse/partner would interpret as loving acts. These loving acts may include, but are not to be limited to, the things you do on special occasions like birthdays, anniversaries, etc. However, the most important loving acts are those little things that you do or might do everyday that say, "I love you. I'm thinking about you." They might include a back rub without being asked, cooking a favorite dinner, or a card or gift for no special reason, etc. Note that the things we listed are things you actively do, not things that you don't do, like not interrupting, not crabbing, etc. Loving is an action word. Do not share this list with your spouse. It is your private list for you to act on or ignore at your discretion.

Exercise 2

In the normal pattern of life of any couple there are many loving acts that each performs that have fallen into the routine of your relationship. This is a bit of the "taking for granted" that is familiar to many people. Being taken for granted is not all bad for this is a part of your commitment to each other, as well as security in the knowledge that each is there for the other for all time. But you each have a need for the other to acknowledge and express appreciation for the special loving, considerate, going-out-of-your-way things that you do. A very loving act is to express, in some way, appreciation for, and sometimes just awareness of, the loving acts your partner does for you. This should never be routinized.

We ask that each of you search your memories for some of these seemingly insignificant and yet cumulatively important acts your spouse/partner does for you that you have grown to expect without comment in your relationship. As in Exercise 1, we ask that you make and keep your list to yourself. Any commitment you make as to whether or not you will express appreciation in the future should also be kept to yourself. It is not appropriate either to confess "your sins of omissions" or to make public resolutions about future behavior. It is appropriate for you personally to decide whether or not you choose to act on your insights.

Exercise 3

This time each of you is to make a list of those things that you would like the other to do for you that you would experience as loving acts. Again, loving is an active verb. On your list there should be no "Stop doing _____." We suggest your list include only statements like the following: "I would appreciate it if you would call when you are going to be late," or "It would be nice if you would let me have fifteen minutes private time when I return home from work."

Your list should also reflect your knowledge and consideration of your partner. For example, you might want to include, "I would like it if you tell me you love me." However, while you might like this, your knowledge of your partner may suggest that this would be out of character for him/her. We ask that you respect this. Your list is to be both selfish and considerate. We hope it will be a beginning for small changes in your lives with each other. It cannot be and should not be an attempt to deal with all the grievances you may have accumulated over the years. Keep your list short and include only what is realistic and doable.

At the end of your list write something like the following: "I would like it if you could do the things I wrote on this list. I fully appreciate that some of them may be difficult for you to do. I know that you may already do some of them some of the time. I guess I am just asking that you do them more frequently. I also know that you will not remember to do all of them all of the time. I know I can't, and I certainly don't expect that of you."

When both of your lists are complete within the guidelines set forth above, arrange a time and a place to meet to exchange the lists made in Exercise 3. Do not discuss them. In exchanging your lists, you will each take a risk in an attempt to improve your relationship. The taking of this risk is the most loving act of all. Respect the risk your partner is taking and receive his/her list in that spirit.

Chapter 7

Comings and Goings

There are many ways to punctuate the phases in the passage of time that we generally describe as a day in the life of a couple or family. We can punctuate it in terms of morning, afternoon, and evening; in terms of breakfast, lunch, and dinner; in terms of the accomplishment of chores to be done such as before work, during work, and after work intervals. We may use any of the above or others as we think about our days. Indeed, it is inevitable that we will do so as we order and make sense of our lives.

In this essay we wish to give you yet another way to think about your days and the days of the people in your lives. We suggest you think in terms of the number of times that you join and part each day. For example, leaving for work is a parting and coming home from work is a joining. These are macro, or large view, partings and joinings. However, each day is also filled with many micro, or small, partings and joinings. Going shopping, going for a run, going to the kitchen, going out to work in the yard, and answering the phone are all small partings. Returning from these and other activities constitutes small joinings.

While partings and joinings are thus constant activities in your lives, we would like you to focus on how they take place. To this end we offer the following principle:

How you part and how you join sets the emotional tone for the next interval in your relationship.

To illustrate, perhaps one partner is greeted by the other on his/her return from work with, "It's about time you got home. It has been a terrible day and I need help!" Such a greeting certainly creates a particular atmosphere for the period of time to follow. Perhaps one partner returns from work and greets the other with, "Who left the rake in the middle of the yard? How many times must I tell people in this house to put things away!" Again the emotional tone, probably conflictual, is set for the rest of the evening and the likelihood of an unpleasant next parting is also increased. These joinings have occurred in ways that are counterproductive to good feelings and pleasurable experiences.

Similarly, one partner may part with, "And I expect you to have that task completed by the time I return!", making it highly likely that negative feelings will dominate the interval before the next joining and the memory of this parting will influence how that joining happens.

We leave you to ponder the different ways you may part and join. Perhaps the best way to stimulate you to imagine the different ways to do so would be to have you ask yourself, "How would I like to be greeted at each joining?" and "What kind of send-off would I like to have each time we part?"

Chapter 8

Making Ordinary Magic

All children engage in magical thinking. And certainly there is something magical about the way children respond as they mature and develop. They are amazed and delighted by each new thing they can do. As they learn to whistle, they do so incessantly. As they learn to walk, talk, ride a bike, or whatever, they engage in each activity with joy, awe, and gusto. Indeed, children seem to approach every aspect of life with a sort of wonder about the magical things that will be revealed to them and a curiosity about the new opportunities that lie ahead. They seek adventures and are disappointed when each day does not provide them with an experience to feed their hunger for the excitement of living.

As we grow older we tend to accept as routine the doing and discovering that were once such a source of wonder. But there is often a part of us that continues to be a "closet" wonderer. We may engage in magical thinking and from time to time wish that we could become Merlin or Samantha and by waving a wand or twitching a nose make the impossible possible. Thus, while adulthood can dull our sense of wonder and our desire for magic, it probably does not eliminate it entirely. We all have our private fantasy lives.

The good news is that there are many things we can do as adults that will lead to magical results. There are also ways to make our private fantasies not only public but also realities. We can create a life that is vital and full of wonder once again. We can release the child in us who has been suppressed by expectations about behaving appropriately adult (i.e., with maturity, dignity, and devoid of fun and excitement).

There are magical words we can use to transform relationships. These magical words may include the following:

- "Could you please help me with..."
- "Thank you very much."
- "I appreciate your help, especially since I know this is not your favorite thing to do."
- "I am sad that things did not work out the way you had hoped they would."
- "I am so excited and happy for you!"
- "Can I help?"
- "How can I help?"

There are also magical gestures we can use to transform relationships. These magical gestures may include the following:

- A foot rub.
- A back rub.
- Doing a chore for your spouse/partner without being asked because you know she/he is busy.
- Listening silently and empathetically.
- Respecting the need for privacy.
- Bringing home a surprise, not necessarily expensive, gift for no special reason.
- Preparing a special celebration for a family member to acknowledge an accomplishment, however small.

Whole households can be transformed by the smell of baking bread, the sound of music, the glow of candles or a fire in the fireplace, by blowing up balloons and letting them float throughout the house, or by blowing bubbles instead of doing the dishes.

The list of things one might do to make ordinary magic is limited only by one's imagination and sense of adventure. We know that each of you has the capacity for magical behavior. You did it as children and it merely lies dormant, waiting to be discovered anew. It is even more fun if you can be childlike and not care how other "adults" react when they observe you. We predict that they will be envious and may even do some experimenting on their own (without telling you, of course).

Chapter 9

The Joy of Touch

Whether it's holiday time or just your normal everyday routine, life can be very hectic. Amidst all the hustle and bustle, comings and goings, work, school, staying in contact with family and friends, shopping, cooking, cleaning, etc., a few moments together, a brief respite for you as a couple can be very important and very much appreciated. We would like to invite you to spend these moments and be energized by the life-giving force of nonsexual touching.

Research has shown that we all have a need for touch, what Sidney Simon has called a "skin hunger." Indeed, babies deprived of adequate personal contact do not develop normally. It also has been demonstrated that touch can have a positive effect on both the intellectual and emotional development of children. Therapeutic touching has become an important aspect of care in all the helping professions. It can help to relieve pain, reduce anxiety, and just plain make us feel better about ourselves and our world. Is it any wonder then that a pat on the shoulder, a neck massage, or a back rub feels so good? Not only do these touches convey a message of caring, but they also fulfill a basic need for human contact.

Sometimes, when we are not conscious of our need for touch, or don't know how to have this need met, we go about getting contact in less appropriate ways. For example, misbehaving children often get spanked as a punishment. But we have found in therapy that having parents rock their children on a regular basis sometimes helps to improve behavior problems enormously. And have you ever noticed how much adolescent males, in particular, are given to punching, slapping, wrestling, etc.? We suspect that, at least in part, this behavior is a response to a continuing need for touch at a time when hugs and similar displays of affection are definitely not "cool." Fortunately, most of us manage to grow up and even to survive adolescence. But unfortunately, we sometimes fail to realize what we knew instinctively as small children, that being touched and held provides us with some of our most nurturing experiences.

In the early days of courtship and marriage we usually can't get enough of touching each other. Lovemaking is usually also at its peak during this period, and thus our skin hunger is more than satisfied. As the years go by, however, life's pressures tend to increase while sexual energies decrease and yet we still need contact with our loved ones every day. We refer here to nonsexual contact, which needs to occur regardless of the level of sexual contact in our relationships. But even as adults we sometimes try to satisfy our skin hunger in inappropriate ways. Thus we nag or complain: "You only kiss me when you want sex!" or "Why don't you want to hold my hand anymore?" Such complaints, however, are rarely likely to get us what we want, which is more physical contact. Rather, in order to achieve this goal, we feel it is important to build touching into the relationship.

In the first place, we recommend hugs on a daily basis, which can be properly given and received even in the midst of the most hectic schedules. But make it a real hug, one with full body contact that lasts at least 30 seconds. And for those times when it is possible to take a half hour to be alone, we offer the following exercises for your enjoyment, as well as for the well-being of you and your relationship.

Exercise 1

Make sure that you are in a quiet place where you will not be disturbed. Sit facing each other with knees touching, either on two chairs or Indian-style on the floor, bed, or couch. Take a few moments to be quiet together, to look at each other, to smile, giggle, be embarrassed, or whatever. Now, first one and then the other, take your spouse/partner's hand in both of yours. Look at that hand for a few moments and then, while still holding it in one of your hands, gently run your fingers up and down your spouse's hand, turning it over from time to time. As you look at and touch that hand, think of all the loving ways it has been used for you and your family. Remember the first time you held that hand and compare it with the way it feels today. Silently thank your spouse/partner for his/her commitment to walk hand in hand through life with you. Give that hand a gentle kiss.

Exercise 2

Take a few minutes before going on to this exercise. Remember, this is not a time for hurrying. This time, first one and then the other, sit on the couch or on the floor leaning against something for support while the other lies face-up in your lap. Now gently stroke the face in your lap, touching all the little nooks and crannies. Gently massage the brows and the cheek area, letting your fingers express your desire to care for the person whose head you are cradling in your lap. When it is your turn to have your face held and touched, you may either close your eyes or look into the eyes of your spouse/partner. But in either case, allow yourself to sink back, relax, and experience fully these touching moments.

Some of you may have decided that the above exercises were not for you. If you did them, we hope you experienced satisfaction and a sense of closeness. In either case, it is likely that there was a difference in each of your responses. One member of a couple may have felt more comfortable with touching in this manner than the other. However, it is not a deficit or a fault on the part of those who felt less comfortable; it is only a difference. As in many aspects of your relationship, the acceptance of and living with difference is one measure of the quality of your life together. Acceptance of difference allows you to feel free to be who you are. And in feeling free you may learn to appreciate even more the joy of touching and being touched.

Chapter 10

Just for Fun

A recurring theme we hope comes through to you as you read this series of essays is that it is important to have fun. In effect, our message is that life, relationships, marriages, and families are too important to be taken seriously all of the time. Accordingly, we have learned a variety of ways to help couples have fun, to enjoy each other, and be creative about having fun. In this essay there are no morals, no examinations of yourself, your spouse/partner, or your relationship. Rather, we share a few "laws" we have collected over the years. Do with them as you will. We intend no lessons and if you read some into them, it is your own doing.

A FEW LAWS OF LIFE AND LIVING

Agnes Allen's Law: Almost anything is easier to get into than out of.
(The wife of Yale historian Frederick Lewis Allen)

Allen's Distinction: The lion and the calf shall lie down together, but the calf won't get much sleep.
(Woody Allen)

Anthony's Law of Force: Don't force it, get a larger hammer.
(Anonymous)

Army Axion: An order that can be misunderstood, will be misunderstood.

Bernstein's Law: A falling body always rolls to the most inaccessible spot.
(Theodore Bernstein)

Bolton's Law of Ascending Budgets: Under current practices, both expenditures and revenues rise to meet each other, no matter which is the largest.
(Joe Bolton)

Boyle's Law: If not controlled, work will flow to the competent person until she/he submerges.
(Charles Boyle)

Broder's Law: Anybody who wants the presidency so much that he'll spend two years organizing and campaigning for it is not to be trusted with the office.
(David Broder)

Canada Bill Jones' Motto: It is morally wrong to allow suckers to keep their money.
(Anonymous)

Dirksen's Three Laws of Politics: (1) Get elected. (2) Get reelected. (3) Don't get mad, get even.
(Everett Dirksen)

Ettore's Observation: The other line moves faster.
(Barbara Ettore)

Getty's First Law: The meek shall inherit the earth, but not its mineral rights.
(J. Paul Getty)

Herblock's Law: If it's good, they'll stop making it.
(Herbert Block)

Hull's Warning: Never insult an alligator until after you have crossed the river.
(Cordell Hull)

Jacquin's Postulate: No man's life, liberty, or property are safe while the legislature is in session.
(Anonymous)

Marshall's Generalized Iceberg Theorem: Seven-eights of everything cannot be seen.
(Anonymous)

Merrill's Maxim of Instant Status: In a democracy you can be respected though poor, but don't count on it.
(Charles Merrill Smith)

Another of Murphy's Laws: It is impossible to make anything foolproof, because fools are so ingenious.
(Anonymous)

Runyon's Law: The race is not always to the swift nor the battle to the strong, but that's the way to bet.
(Damon Runyon)

First Law of Wing-Walking: Never leave hold of what you've got until you've got hold of something else.
(Donald Herzberg).

Okay, so what's the moral and the lesson? Believe it or not, there is none. We just wanted to give you a respite from "working at it." Enjoy! On second thought, there is a moral: take time to smell the flowers, laugh, and share trivia with your spouse/partner, family, and friends.

We will conclude by giving you a puzzle to solve. Perhaps this too is for fun, but perhaps there is a moral or lesson. Below we present nine dots. They are to be connected with four straight lines without lifting the pencil from the paper.

THE NINE-DOT PROBLEM

```
*    *    *

*    *    *

*    *    *
```

We present no solution to this problem. Perhaps in another essay you will learn of the solution, if there is one.

Chapter 11

Acceptance

R espect for difference is a frequent general theme throughout this book. In this essay, however, we focus specifically on respecting differences, but we choose to give it a different name. We choose to call it acceptance.

Often acceptance is a very rare experience in our lives. However, we all seek it, and when we experience acceptance, we value it and the person with whom we have the experience very highly. Professionals in the field of marriage and family counseling have identified acceptance as a key component in successful marriages/relationships. In fact, acceptance is a basic building block for strong relationships. Strangely enough, it is only through acceptance of things as they are that your relationship can evolve to fit the changing circumstances of your life together.

Many problems emerge in a marriage/relationship when we try consciously to get the other person to change, to be different, to be the kind of spouse/partner we think he or she should be. For, counter to logic, conscious attempts to change another usually serve only to maintain that person where she/he is. That is, when you attempt to change someone, that person will probably not only resist but will also attempt reciprocally to change you. Ultimately, a pattern emerges in which each person attempts to get the other to quit trying to change him/her. By contrast, and also counter to logic, if we accept people as they are, they cannot stay the same.

Unfortunately, we are besieged on a daily basis with ideas from the "experts" in the human science professions about how our relationships are "supposed to be." Magazines, popular press books, radio, and television have become a constant source of advice. Although well-intentioned, this information and advice may become the source of problems rather than of their solution as we consciously try to reshape our relationships or question the validity of what we are doing.

Indeed, in a very real sense, our writing this essay on acceptance implies that we are consciously trying to change you to be more accepting of your spouse/partner, and because of this it is not likely to be successful! You may read this essay, you may nod your head in agreement with the logic of the illogical idea that one can get change through acceptance, and yet we know realistically that the idea may not be implemented by you.

We are also flipping around the idea of acceptance pretty loosely. So let's try to define it a bit. Acceptance does not necessarily mean liking what your spouse/partner does. It means living with your spouse as she/he is. Acceptance implies that you are okay enough about yourself and flexible enough to not need other people in general and your spouse/partner in particular to be a certain way with you. Thus, acceptance of your spouse/partner depends very strongly on how good you feel about yourself. In acceptance, there is gentleness and respect toward yourself just as there is gentleness and respect for the other.

Acceptance of ourselves, however, is often very difficult. In our culture we have been taught that we must always try to improve, to be better, and to get rid of our faults. We tend to be very critical of ourselves. Most of us were reared in families in which we learned more about what we did wrong than what we did right. And so we internalized a critical attitude toward ourselves. Such an attitude is often manifested not only in a focus on the negative in others but also in our embarrassment at accepting compliments about our own behavior. We respond by saying, "Yes, but I should have or I could have done it even better," when a simple "thank you" would do very nicely.

Moreover, we tend to bring this style of relating to others into our mar-riages/relationships. Both you and your spouse/partner may learn more from each other about what you do wrong as husband, wife, or partner than about what you do right. You may blame your spouse/partner for your lack of success in being the way you think you should be: "I would be okay if only she/he would _____." And so many marriages/relationships evolve into a series of reciprocal exchanges in which one tries to get the other to be the way one wants the other to be so one can be the way she/he thinks he/she is "supposed to be."

But that's enough talk! Let's get to some exercises that may be useful to you in assessing yourself, your spouse/partner, and your relationship, and hopefully may lead to greater acceptance in each.

Exercise 1

Make a personal inventory of yourself as you see yourself and as you see others seeing you. There should be several parts to this list, and we ask you to write a complete description of each aspect of yourself upon which you choose to focus. Sample items are presented below:

I worry. I have tried for a long time not to be such a worrier. However, I have never succeeded in stopping my worrying, even though people have told me that I shouldn't or have no need to worry. I guess I am stuck being a worrier. I know I am not particularly fun to be around when I worry, but that is the way I am, and it's probably a part of who I will always be. I'll have to live with my worrying, and people in my life will have to live with me the way I am. I can accept my worrying. I have to accept the fact that others do not like it when I worry because that is their right also.

I am super-organized. I like a clean, neat house and life. I like to have plans. I know people find my super-organization hard to accept and live with. Yet, that is my choice. People have the right not to like it and not be super-organized like myself. I'll have to accept the fact that that's the way I am, that we each make different choices, and that we may always have disagreements about what level of organization is acceptable.

I am a good parent. I am firm and yet loving. I have always been this way, and I probably always will be this way. My children will get angry with me from time to time, and sometimes my spouse/partner will think I am too firm. But I believe that my loving balances my firmness and that my children will love me and respect me for the way I am, even though they may not always like it.

Now you try. Do a reasonably complete inventory of yourself. And feel free to add to it from time to time. You are the way you are. You probably always will be that way, and that's the way it is. We are reasonably sure it will be more comfortable for you to do an inventory of your "faults" as opposed to your "virtues." But we invite you to accept that discomfort and to include some of your virtues as well as those things about yourself you find less than desirable.

Exercise 2

Now let's do an inventory of your spouse/partner as you might experience him/her in the context of acceptance. Again, we'll give you some examples:

George is a quiet, reserved person who does not share his feelings very easily. It would be nice if he did, but he never has, and probably never will do so. I don't like it this way, but I need to accept the fact that George will probably always be this way in spite of my best efforts to change him. I probably will always keep trying to change George, and George will probably always resist and stay the same. I guess I'll have to live with things this way.

Louise is a very sensitive, understanding woman. She listens well to what I have to say and always considers me and involves me in the decisions she makes. I really like this. She probably always will be this way, and I will probably always appreciate it. That's the way I am with her, that's the way she is with me, that's the way we are in this relationship, and it's nice.

Once again, it's now your turn. Remember to include in your inventory of your spouse/partner those aspects of him/her you experience as positives as well as those that have a negative impact on you.

Exercise 3

And now we suggest an experiment. Perhaps for an hour a day (no more than that, please), pretend that you can accept those parts of yourself you have trouble accepting. When people are critical of you, try responding without apology: "Yes, you're right. I probably shouldn't... (worry, be this organized, like football as much as I do, etc.) or probably should... (express my feelings more freely, etc.), but that's the way I have always been and the way I probably always will be. I know you don't like it. I know that you will probably try to change this part of me, but I doubt very much that I or you will be successful. But thanks for caring enough to tell me how you feel."

A second experiment (again, for no more than an hour a day) is to accept the person who is your spouse/partner as she/he is—a worrier, watcher of football games, a person who has difficulty accepting feelings, or whatever. As best you can, simply acknowledge that this is the way she/he is and that you can accept this as a fact of life. If you can accept your spouse/partner as he/she is, and if you can accept yourself as you are, you will experience the magic of acceptance and the little differences that will evolve in your relationship as a function of changes in your behavior.

In our culture we are constantly admonished to be all that we can be. The hardest part of this is feeling free to be who we are. Until we experience this freedom, all that we can be will most likely remain an ever elusive goal.

Chapter 12

Grief and Mourning

Intellectually we may acknowledge the fact of our immortality, but emotionally we probably would agree with Woody Allen, who said, "I don't want to achieve immortality through my work. I want to achieve it through not dying." However, a normal part of the growth process is to feel an increasing acceleration of our movement toward the inevitability of death. Indeed, the experience of the passage of time is not absolute; rather, it is relative to age. Impatience with how slowly time passes seems reserved for youth, and we curse its speed as we get older. Yet death is a part of living. It is a part of the continuity of life as older generations give way to the new, just as winter must give way to spring.

The sadness and grief we experience upon the death of a person who is important to us in our lives is a reminder of the importance of relationships in our lives. A void is created, never to be filled by another person. For each relationship has its own special meaning that is exclusive to that person. A death is also a reminder of our own mortality and a time for reflection on the meaning and purpose of our lives. The grief and sadness we experience seem to be different relative to the nature of the relationship we had with the person who died. In a quality relationship, we grieve our loss, but it is tempered with memories of the happy things we did together or meaningful moments we shared with that person. If the relationship did not include many happy activities or meaningful moments shared, the grief contains aspects of regret, mourning not only of the loss, but of opportunities missed. But, whatever its nature, the grief and mourning must occur. This is a part of living, a part of being people who can think and conceptualize our own nonexistence. Living or dying is not a choice available to us.

On the other hand, how we live, how we prepare ourselves through myriad opportunities available to us is a choice we can make. Erik Erikson suggested that people who live meaningful, productive lives in caring, intimate relationships experience their impending deaths very differently and thus affect the generations that follow in significant ways.

There are context markers or stages in the lives of individuals and families that are built-in moments for the opportunity to reflect on our lives and to make conscious decisions about how we might learn to make our lives more meaningful and productive. Just as there is sadness at the death of a friend, there is a certain sadness experienced at points of transition. Entry into a new stage marks the passage of time and the end of the previous stage. However, each transition is an opportunity and a challenge to move on to the next stage with, perhaps, a renewed commitment to make the new one better than the last. As the challenges of each stage are met, the passage to the next stage is less fraught with regret as an accompaniment to the necessary sadness.

Some family transition points are described below. As you read through each, reflect on your own experience at that moment of your life. Examine the degree of satisfaction you felt with your efforts in the stage preceding this point. Consider what you might do to enrich the next stage in your life.

FAMILY TRANSITION POINTS

The Child Leaves Home
The emotional issue here is accepting parent-offspring separation. This is a major turning point in the life of a family. As a young adult, how did you feel about your experience in your family of origin? How did you feel about leaving home? As a parent, how did you feel when your child left home or how do you feel about that prospect? What is the nature of your relationship with each child?

The Newly Married/Committed Couple
The issue here is commitment, sharing, and giving. As the older generation, you experience your child where you once were, embarking on a new life. As the younger generation, you may ask what your parents gave you in preparation for this beginning of a new life? How will both generations support their children?

Childbearing
The issue here is making room for and accepting responsibility for a new, helpless family member, while simultaneously nurturing your marriage/relationship. The joy of having a child is tempered somewhat with sadness at the passage of the previous two stages. Did you experience a sense of loss? What can you do to recapture your coupleness?

The School-Age Child

The child's going to school is the first rehearsal for his/her ultimate separation. Again, we mourn the loss of the early years together. How can we make the best use of this stage of exploration and expansion into the world?

Teenage Child

In this stage we are confronted with the fact that the young person will ultimately leave home. We anticipate the beginning of a life without children in the family. How can we prepare ourselves for being alone again? What kind of attention can we now give each other? What are the demands of our careers and our own parents?

The Child Leaves Home

We have come full circle. You experience what your parents experienced. You experience yourself as older and growing older more quickly. How can we make the most of the time left to us? What kind of career and relationship goals will be attained?

Middle-Age Parents

The issue here is creating a good marriage/relationship without children. You are no longer who you were when first you were married or made a permanent commitment. The challenge is to relate in a different way. How will you deal with your own aging parents? How will you assess the quality of that relationship?

Retirement

A new adjustment, a new challenge, a life without infinite future, although this is a period of increasing length as people live longer. Here we face the meaningfulness of our lives and the quality of the relationships in our lives. What will you feel as you assess your life? What changes can you still make to achieve a sense of satisfaction and integration?

Each stage seems to combine both excitement and sadness. Successful passage through and meeting of the challenges characteristic of each stage prepare us for the next stage and ultimately prepare us and our children for the final stage of growth, our deaths. You cannot go back and relive each stage. You can, however, go back to each important relationship in your life and own responsibility for your part in what it is not, what it might have been, and what it might still be. With the death of each stage in your life, you will grieve its passage. We hope you can also learn the lessons that each stage has to teach and the promise that each offers you.

Chapter 13

Genogram: Another Piece of the Puzzle

We would like to talk with you about the families in which each of you grew up and the role of these families in your marriage/relationship. Then we will describe a method for creating a map, or genogram, of your family that may help you get a fresh look at your marriage/relationship and what each of you brings to it.

We always feel it is important to point out that when two people make a permanent commitment, it is more the joining of two families than of two individuals. A funny idea, you say? Well, maybe, but let's think about it for a minute. Each of you (and us) was born into a family of one sort or another. In that family you learned the basic rules for living, according to which you operated, at least until you became aware of those rules and decided either to rebel against them, make choices about them, and/or create your own.

For example, from the moment of your birth, you began to learn how love and affection were to be given and received, how feelings were to be handled, how fathers father, how mothers mother, how moms and dads, brothers and sisters relate to each other, what behaviors were and were not acceptable. Indeed, the list is as long as the number of things your family did or didn't do, or believed you should or shouldn't do. Although such guidelines were rarely openly expressed, they were the implicit rules and values of your family. And the way they became very explicit was when your behavior violated one of these rules, because then you were sure to hear about it!

For a long time you probably assumed that the way your family operated was the way it was in every family. The reality is, however, that every family is unique. Every family has its own set of shoulds and shouldn'ts, and it is the particular set of rules and patterns characteristic of each family that helps to define that family's uniqueness. Further, each set of behavioral rules is embedded in a distinct family/historical context that colors their present impact, despite the fact that the original meanings may have long since been forgotten or lost. Such shadings may have derived from a particular religious pattern or ethnic heritage, from health-related experiences, economic realities, and/or social and cultural influences. Thus, although families may share similar rules, such rules may have a different meaning or message in each family. Therefore, as a child who grew up in the particular family that you did, you fell heir to a set of traditions, both implicit and explicit, that has influenced and been influenced by each of the generations that preceded you.

Each spouse/partner brings this inheritance with him or her into the new marriage/relationship. And part of the challenge facing the new couple is how to blend the rules and traditions brought from each family of origin, how to create those that will be characteristic of this new relationship, and how to define a family that is uniquely their own. Step one in dealing with this challenge is to recognize and accept each other's differences, not only in terms of the obvious individual and family characteristics, but also in terms of the implicit rules on how a family "should" operate that each learned.

One way of getting a better understanding of the territory from which you hail is to draw a family map on which you plot as much information as you know about your family of origin. This map is called a genogram, and it may help you not only to get to know yourselves and each other better, but it may also send you out to do some research among other members of your family as you find some gaps in your knowledge.

Exercise 1

Plan a time and a place where you can be alone together for about an hour. You will need a large sheet of paper and a pencil. You may want to take a cup of coffee or another beverage with you. However, be sure to turn off the television and take the phone off the hook. Hang an imaginary "Do Not Disturb" sign outside your private space and remember that it should be violated only in the case of an emergency.

A genogram is not unlike a family tree. The difference is that you are able to include more information. Relationships of the same generation are indicated by horizontal lines and offspring are indicated by vertical lines. We draw circles for females and squares for males (you can make of that what you want), and we like to include at least three generations. A horizontal line with a slash through it indicates a divorce, a triangle with a question mark in it indicates a pregnancy, and a death is indicated by placing a large X on that person's circle, square, or triangle (for miscarriage or stillborn). List oldest children to youngest children by going from left to right. The genogram symbols are illustrated below:

GENOGRAM SYMBOLS

Now, before you get too confused, look at the example of our family. From this simple drawing you can learn a great deal about us. You can see, for example, that Dorothy was the third of four children and Ray was the fourth of four children. Each had very different backgrounds, both in terms of family structure (both of Ray's parents had died by the time he was 14) and geographical location (urban vs. rural). Dorothy came into the marriage with two children and had been divorced, while Ray had never been married before. And recent years have been marked by some major losses.

Now you try it. After you have drawn the basics, fill in everything you know about each family. Include such things as first names and family names, geographical locations, religions, occupations, diseases from which family members suffered or died, current ages or age at time of death, dates of marriages and divorces, special skills or talents, and anything else you can think of that helps to describe your families.

GENOGRAM OF RAY AND DOROTHY BECVAR

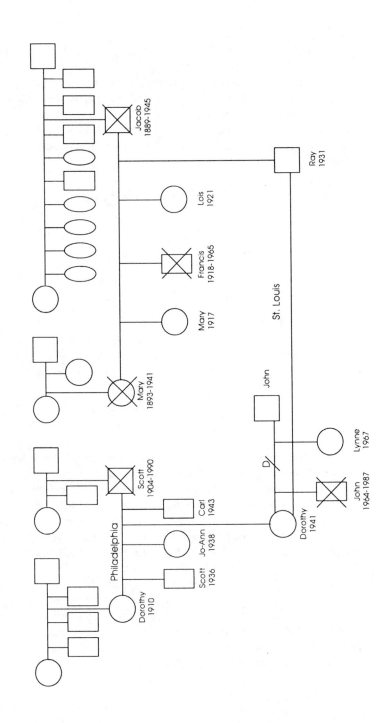

After you have done this, spend some time talking about the ways in which your families were alike and were different. Spend some time appreciating the unique heritage each of you has brought to your marriage relationship. Be grateful for both the negatives and the positives and for the fact that neither of you would be the person you are today without this particular heritage.

Chapter 14

Understanding Your Families of Origin

Perhaps the most universal of experiences is to be born into a family. This was the primary setting in which you learned about yourself, about the world, about getting along with others, etc. However, most people would describe these experiences as bittersweet. For some their experiences tilt more toward the bitter as they reflect back upon their childhoods. For others, memories are marked mostly by the sweet. Indeed, neutral feelings as people recall their experiences of growing up are almost nonexistent.

One of the ongoing themes in the field of psychotherapy is the phenomenon of blaming parents for whatever has gone wrong in the life of the child. One might even describe current theories and practices of psychotherapy as being engaged in full-fledged parent bashing. This is reflected in the various adult children of _____ syndromes, in which the theme is one of "I am the way I am because my parents did this, did not do that, did not do enough of that, or did too little of this." And perhaps this is true; perhaps our experiences would be very different if our parents had been different. What is significant, however, is that most of these theories tell us that the solutions lie in securing professional help in order to learn to live with the "baggage with which you have been burdened." A parallel to this trend is the conscious effort on the part of today's parents to do it right so that "our children will not experience themselves, the world, and others as we do." Many parents currently are working to be a counterforce to their own personal experiences as children. And they are aided and abetted in their desire to prevent problems by the various offerings of professionals: parenting classes or workshops, hundreds of manuals and books on parenting, and/or the advice to seek counseling or therapy. The "experts" take the forefront once again, whether directly or indirectly.

While not defending parents from any generation, it is our purpose to remind you that your parents brought a legacy from their own families of origin to their marriage/relationship and to the families in which you grew up. They reared you in a context characterized by both joys and struggles, not unlike those you yourself may be experiencing today. Parent bashing without perspective on your parents, their dreams, lives, heritage, reality, pains, and joys is therefore unfair. Some important questions need to be asked, including: Did your parents do the best they could in the particular context and historical period in which they were operating? Could your parents have done better? Would your parents wish they had done better?

The activity we suggest with this essay is designed to help you gain a perspective on your parents. The issue is not forgiveness. Rather, the issue is understanding the context of your parents' lives together given their personal legacies from their families of origin in the historical period in which they lived and in which they were reared.

This is an activity for each of you to do alone because each of you had your own set of parents. We will ask you to use a variety of means to understand your parents in a way that you as a child could not understand. In the process of trying to understand your parents we ask that you suspend judgment of them until you gain the perspective of their lives and stories.

Exercise 1

We suggest that you meet informally and separately with each of your parents if they are still living. Approach them with an attitude of seeking to understand rather than one of inquisition. A lunch or walk together is often far better than a formal interview format. One or both of your parents may be reluctant to self-disclose, but with nonjudgmental interest in their stories you may be more successful than you believe possible. If one or both of your parents has died, other family members may be a good source of information about them—an uncle, an aunt, a cousin, a hunting buddy. One of your siblings may also provide important information, but you must remember that their experience of your parents may be very different from yours. (The family experience of no two siblings is ever the same, for you quite literally grew up in two different families based on the point at which you arrived and who was already there.)

Try to get inside your parents, to "walk in their shoes," so to speak. Try to feel what it felt like to be your Mom and Dad during your years in the family, and what it feels like to be your Mom and Dad at this stage of their lives as they reflect back over the years. Again, suspend judgment. Understand!

A question that continually intrigues us is, "What kind of experience is the right experience for us to have had, and what kind of experience is right for our children?" Our answers are many and varied for there is no one right answer. Further, we believe it is important to recognize the valuable aspects of each different experience and the opportunities for learning and growth each has provided.

Chapter 15

Building Your Marriage/Family Chronology

In this essay we again invite each of you to venture into your personal past as well as into the history of your relationship so that you may better understand your experience of yourself and each other in the present. We all experience the passing of time as too fast or too slow depending upon the things that are going on in our lives. Children and adolescents "can't wait" to get older. And then around the age of 30 we often experience a reversal; we feel "we are getting older too quickly." Between 30 and 40 we begin to count the years until our death rather than the years from our birth. And with each passing year, the pace seems to quicken and soon the years merge, one into another.

As we look back on our lives, it seems to be a universal feeling that time has passed very quickly. Viewed retrospectively, all the years and events in our lives are remembered as happening yesterday. Yet one could say also that all of the years and the events that shaped our lives continue to live in us in the "now." For the events of each day, week, and year influence the kind of person we are today. Edgar Auerswald described this as the "event-shape in time-space," and it will be the focus of our exercise for you and your partner in this essay. This can be a very meaningful and fun experience that you may also want to share with your children. Together you can create individual and family histories, perhaps allowing you to understand yourself, your spouse/partner, and your relationship in different and more meaningful ways.

Exercise 1

Plan a time and place where you can be alone together for about an hour. You will need a large sheet of paper and a pencil. Again, you may want to include refreshments. Be sure to turn off the television and take the phone off the hook. This is your private time and politely yet firmly let others know that you are not to be disturbed unless there is an emergency.

In another essay you were invited to do a genogram. If you completed that exercise, we hope that you learned more about your family and each of your families of origin. In this exercise you will add to your knowledge by doing individual and family chronologies. A chronology is a time line on which you record the events you recall as important in your individual development and in the development of your relationship/family. You may notice that what consti-tutes an important event may be very different for each of you. And sometimes you may find that events that seemed insignificant at the time have become very important in retrospect. As you record each event, share your memory of the event and the meaning you assign to your experience of the event. We present a piece of our individual and family chronologies to illustrate how you can do your own. Because of space limitations we include only highlights of our histories. First a bit of our individual chronologies:

Raphael J. Becvar   **Dorothy Stroh Becvar**

October 24, 1931. Born to Jacob and Mary Becvar in Calmar, Iowa. (St. Raphael's day)

1937. Spent five months with mother in Los Angeles, CA.

1939. Ring bearer for sister Mary's wedding.

March 1941. Mother died.   *March 14, 1941. Born to Dorothy and Muir Stroh in Philadelphia, PA.*

October 1941. Regina became housekeeper for my Dad and me.

August 1943. My Dad and I moved to Decorah, Iowa.

November 1944. Younger brother born. Moved to larger home.

June 1945. My Father died.

June 1945. My sister Mary and her husband took me into their family on their farm.

1946. "Mysterious" illness. Spent summer in bed while three siblings were sent to be with grandmother.

1950. Graduated From H.S.

1950. Entered Loras College.

1951. Went to summer camp for one week.

1953. Confirmation in the Lutheran Church.

1954. Began teaching in Iowa.

1959. Moved to a second job in Iowa.

1959. Graduated from H.S.

1963. Entered graduate school in Nebraska.

1963. Graduated from Cornell U. Married and moved to Boston.

1964. Birth of son, John.

1965. Entered graduate school in Minnesota.

1967. Birth of daughter, Lynne.

We jump ahead now to share a bit of our family chronology so that you can see how this is done:

October 1976. Dorothy and Ray met at a Marriage and Family Therapy Conference in Philadelphia.

December 1976. Ray spent Christmas with Dorothy and her children.

1977. Ray started Marriage and Family Development and Therapy Program at St. Louis Unviersity.

June 1978. Put a new roof on Dorothy's house.

August 1978. Married in Pennsylvania. Moved family to St. Louis to Ray's apartment.

November 1978. Moved to our present home.

etc., etc., etc.

Now you try it. The chronology merely punctuates the event-shape in time-space. While certainly important, the meaning and significance of the events are much more important. What did the event at that time, and in those circumstances, mean to you? Share this with each other and perhaps later with your children. Each of you had unique experiences which you brought to your marriage/relationship. You have had many shared experiences in your lives together. Some experiences were negative. Some were positive. All are meaningful. No event-shape is too small. Each may have an important place in your chronology.

Sometimes the seemingly insignificant events have the most profound influences on our lives and families. You may want to add to your chronology from time to time, so you might hang it in an accessible place in your home. You might also help your children build their own personal chronologies to hang next to your family's. To make room for all, you may need to hang the top sheet of paper at ceiling level. Feel free to laugh, cry, be nostalgic, or whatever else seems appropriate. You might make the following entry on your chronology: "Today, _____(date)_____, we built our individual and family chronologies, and we got to know each other better."

Chapter 16

Creating a Family Shield

O ne of the things that we have learned to appreciate more and more over the
years is that while members of a marriage/relationship or family may share
a great deal in common, each is a unique person and that uniqueness needs to
be valued and respected. One way to celebrate both the unique aspects of
individuals and the common bond that members of a marriage/relationship or
family share is to create a Family Shield. We therefore invite you to find a time
when all the members of your family can participate in this activity.

A Family Shield is similar to a coat-of-arms, which is a symbolic repre-
sentation of the standards and values of the family. Typically the coat-of-arms
includes a motto or noble statement, often in Latin, according to which members
of the family are to live. While the Family Shield symbolically represents the
common values that the whole family shares, it also allows space for each
member to represent his/her uniqueness.

For this activity you will need newsprint or a poster board, pencils, colored
magic markers and/or crayons. First you must decide on the shape of the shield.
It could be round, star-shaped, rectangular, traditionally shield-shaped, or it
might be nontraditional. For example, if you are Irish, perhaps it might be in the
form of a shamrock. After agreeing upon a shape, sketch it on your newsprint
or poster board. The shield is then divided into sections so that each member
has a space, as well as a space for the family as a whole. Next, each person draws
and colors a symbol to represent him/her in the appropriate space. Finally,
everyone decides on a symbol to represent the family as a whole. This is drawn
in the designated family space along with the family name and/or motto.

To help you get a better idea of what we are suggesting, we present a sample Family Shield for you to see. Remember, however, this illustration depicts a different family. Your family and its individual members are unique. Celebrate this uniqueness. And when you are finished making your Family Shield, you may want to find a place to hang it where you can enjoy your creation.

THE SMITH FAMILY SHIELD

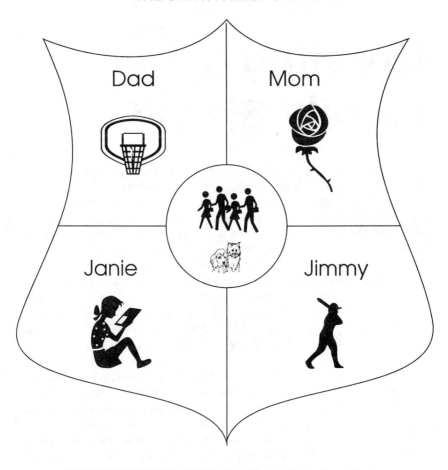

Chapter 17

Resolving Conflicts I

One of the things that the fairy tales don't include with their message, "... and they lived happily ever after," is the fact that happy-ever-aftering doesn't necessarily preclude the possibility of conflict. As you may recall from the preface, we believe that if your relationship is satisfactory 75% of the time, you are doing very well. Obviously that leaves at least 25% of the time when things are less than wonderful. Thus we would say that conflict is inevitable even in the best of relationships. What *is not* inevitable, however, is that conflict must spell disaster. Indeed, successful relationships, marriages, and families are characterized by effective skills for problem solving. Conflicts are acknowledged, dealt with, resolved, and life goes on. And in successful relationships, marriages, and families the members are able to talk about their communication problems and are able to agree to disagree when consensus is not possible.

Some patterns that we have noticed in our work with couples and families are that 1) people in relationships tend to develop a habitual way of trying to solve problems that repeats itself regardless of the issue at hand and that 2) this method may or may not work. Thus, whether the argument is about money, sex, kids, or in-laws, the way a particular couple argues usually looks the same and usually ends up in the same place. And when a couple is having problems with conflict resolution, what we must look at is not the issue, but the pattern they have evolved for dealing with issues.

For example, with one couple the characteristic pattern may be blaming one another; with another couple, dredging up the past invariably happens whenever things get a little hot. We call such patterns the "rules" for arguing that the couple has implicitly agreed will be characteristic of their relationship. In either case, however, the blaming and the dredging get in the way of, indeed prevent, finding a solution for, or at least reaching a compromise on, the issue at hand. And if conflict inevitably leads to an impasse, at best, or open warfare, at worst, it is no wonder that it is so often feared. However, it is not the conflict that must be eliminated. Rather, it is how conflict is dealt with that needs to be focused upon. What needs to change are the rules in the relationship about how to argue and how to solve problems.

Something else that we have noticed in our work is that couples who are successful at conflict resolution are able to talk about how they argue, how they communicate. That is, they are able to acknowledge the rules currently in use, examine them honestly, and revise them when necessary. They have a rule for changing the rules. This ability to look at and talk about the what and the how of their relationship is called metacommunication, and we think that it is one of the keys to building a successful relationship. Therefore, in this essay we would like to help you focus on the way you handle conflict in your relationship and offer some suggestions in the area of metacommunication, which we hope will help you make your relationship as satisfactory as you would like it to be.

As usual, we would like you to agree upon a time and a place where you are comfortable, can be assured of privacy, and will not feel rushed. Sit facing each other, with knees or hands touching if possible. Be sure to make eye contact as much as possible and remember that how you handle conflict is a message about how you feel about one another.

Exercise 1

One of you (partner A) chooses an issue that is of some importance to you but is not a hot topic in your relationship. Take as much time as you need to describe the issue and your feelings about it, while the other (partner B) gives you his/her full attention but says nothing. When you have finished speaking, ask your spouse/partner if he/she has understood what you have just said. Partner B, now paraphrase what partner A has just said and describe what you believe his/her feelings are about the issue. Next, partner A, let partner B know whether his/her perceptions about what you said and felt are accurate. When both sets of perceptions about partner A's position match, reverse the process, with partner B talking about an issue of importance and partner A listening and then checking out what was heard until mutual understanding is reached.

When you have finished this exercise, stop and talk about what you have just done. We predict you felt uncomfortable, possibly embarrassed, and certainly not very spontaneous. But did you also feel listened to and understood? Was speaking without being interrupted a pleasant experience? Did you enjoy being able to stay focused on the issue? Are there some pieces of this method that might be useful in your relationship?

We would suggest you try exercise 1 a few more times before going on to exercise 2.

Exercise 2

This time the topic of discussion will be how you usually argue, your communication "rules." Using the same method as in exercise 1, take turns stating your opinion about what you believe your usual pattern is and how you feel when these rules are operating. Be sure to take turns, giving each other your full attention, making sure you understand one position before you move on to the other. Remember, there is to be no interrupting, no sidetracking, and no arguing about who is right or wrong. Your job is to achieve some understanding about how each of you perceives the way you usually handle conflict.

When you have finished this exercise, talk a little bit about what you learned. Were you surprised? Are there some things you are doing well? Not so well? What would you like to change? Are there some things from these two exercises that you might want to try using the next time you are faced with conflict?

Please be aware that the patterns you have established did not emerge over night but have been evolving since the day you met. Efforts to change should be undertaken slowly and carefully and without any expectations of miracles. Further, if your marriage/relationship is seriously troubled, we would suggest you not try the preceding exercises without professional assistance. Nor should lack of desire to try them be used as a weapon against your spouse/partner. Remember, "different strokes for different folks" and what we suggest is not necessarily right for every couple.

Chapter 18

Resolving Conflicts II

In this essay we take a slightly different approach to conflict resolution. Our focus is on making decisions regarding what is important to fight or argue about. And our goal is to help you reduce the number of issues or events around which the two of you may experience conflict. In our work we frequently hear statements like, "We fight over such trivial, unimportant things!" While we could make several interpretations of this statement and suggest a variety of interventions, we often use it as an opportunity to help a couple make decisions about those issues which are or are not worth the battle.

We begin by explaining that the meaning of any event is relative to the interpretation of that event. It is our belief that each of us has an internal map or conceptual model of events and behaviors according to which such events and behaviors are judged to be either acceptable or unacceptable. This map is our private view of what is "supposed to be" and what is "not supposed to be" and the feelings we feel are relative to whether the event or behavior fits in the former rather than the latter category. Thus, if the behavior of another or ourselves fits what we believe is appropriate, the feeling we experience will be pleasure. Conversely, if the behavior fits what we believe is inappropriate, the feeling will be displeasure. In this way we may understand that what we feel is relative to the meaning ascribed to the behavior.

A logical response upon experiencing an event or behavior that is acceptable is not only to feel pleasure but also to acknowledge that feeling to the other person involved. A logical response upon experiencing an event or behavior that is unacceptable is to feel displeasure and to attempt to correct or change the "deviation" to an event or behavior that is acceptable. And a logical response by the person who is asked to change is to resist or to reciprocate by attempting to change the person who is trying to change him/her, for such attempts to get him/her to change may fall into that person's unacceptable range.

As you and your partner have different maps and therefore interpret events differently, you will also have different feelings about these events. For example, Frank's map may be illustrated as follows:

Not supposed to be Unacceptable	Supposed to be Acceptable	Not supposed to be Unacceptable
Feels displeasure	Feels pleasure	Feels displeasure

According to Frank's map, the range of acceptable behavior is very small. Therefore we might expect from him a high frequency of attempts to change the behavior of others in his world. By contrast, Pauline may have the following very different map:

Not supposed to be Unacceptable	Supposed to be Acceptable	Not supposed to be Unacceptable
Feels displeasure	Feels pleasure	Feels displeasure

For Pauline many more behaviors will fall into the acceptable range. Therefore we might expect from her a higher frequency of feelings of pleasure and fewer attempts to change the behavior of others in her world. In addition, she probably will also experience fewer instances of resistance to change or reciprocal attempts by others to change her.

If Frank and Pauline were in a relationship, we might expect Frank to make more attempts to change Pauline, while Pauline would have greater latitude in her expectations of herself and others. In fact, Frank may work on Pauline to get her to raise her standards, while Pauline may work on Frank to get him to loosen up. Neither is right or wrong; they are just different. Indeed, while the general range of acceptable/unacceptable behaviors may be similar, one rarely finds a relationship in which the members have identical maps. There will almost always be some degree of difference, and it is our opinion that much of this difference is something with which we must learn to live.

A useful definition of conflict, therefore, may be the experience of disagreement or difference between two people having two different conceptual maps who engage in reciprocal attempts to change each other's map and associated feelings. While some conflict is inevitable, we believe that it may be useful for couples to examine their differences and decide which are trivial and which are worthy of continuing attempts to change the other. To that end we suggest doing the following exercises.

Exercise 1

This exercise is to be done by each of you privately. Further, we do not recommend that you share your experience with each other. You will need a notebook and a pencil or pen, as well as a block of time in which to reflect and write.

In part one of this exercise, we ask that you each make a list of those recurring issues in your relationship that suggest you have different conceptual models or maps of acceptable and unacceptable behaviors. Do not discriminate between the important and the trivial in developing your list. The list may include such things as how the other chews his/her food, when she/he comes home from work, drinking behavior, amount of television watching or newspaper reading, amount of time spent on the telephone, how the toothpaste tube is squeezed, etc. Take about half an hour to create your initial list.

In part two of this exercise we ask that as you live with each other for the next week you be in tune with your feelings of pleasure and displeasure. Try to identify the behavior in the other that is associated with each of these feelings. Also, keep your notebook handy and add to the list whenever it seems appropriate. Don't wait too long or you may not recall the event or behavior.

Exercise 2

After the week of tuning in to and observing your spouse/partner, sit down in a quiet place and carefully examine your list. What you might look for are those behaviors/events that are not worthy of the amount of displeasure you have given them in the past. For each behavior/event you might ask yourself, "Is it really worth the hassle?" or "Is this an exercise in futility?" or "Is asking him/her to change this fair of me?" Remember that you may never like the event or behavior in question. The issue is whether or not you can become reconciled to living with it. You might even imagine adopting a different conceptual map similar to the following:

Unacceptable	Can live with	Acceptable	Can live with	Unacceptable
Displeasure	Neutral	Pleasure	Neutral	Displeasure

Our hope is that, as you eliminate some of the more trivial issues from your list, you each may experience a relationship with more freedom from reciprocal attempts to change the other and thus may enjoy each other more.

Now we suggest you do the following two exercises, which focus more directly on yourselves as individuals. Our hope, however, is that they also may help you to experience more satisfaction in your relationship.

Exercise 3

Once again, this exercise is to be done privately and we do not recommend that you share your experiences with each other. With your notebook and pen or pencil and some quiet time, make a list of those behaviors or aspects of yourself about which you feel displeasure. As in exercise 1, do not discriminate between important and trivial in developing this list. The list may include how you procrastinate, how you look, how much you drink, how much you do or don't exercise, how you use the toothpaste, etc. Take about half an hour to create this list. As you live with yourself for the next week, be in tune with your feelings of pleasure and displeasure with yourself about what you do, don't do, should do more or less of, etc. Keep your notebook handy and add to the list whenever it is appropriate.

Exercise 4

After the week of tuning in to and observing yourself, sit down in a quiet place and carefully examine your list. In examining your list, you might ask yourself, "Is it worth the hassle?" or "Is this an exercise in futility?" or "Is it fair to keep beating myself up about this?" or "Could I modify my map about what my 'supposed to be' is in this regard?" Note that you may never like certain behaviors that you do. However, after many attempts to change yourself over the years, it may be time to reconcile yourself to living with who you are, even if you don't necessarily like it.

We suspect that as you are easier on yourself, you may find more joy and pleasure in the person that you are. And, of course, if you can enhance your capacity to enjoy yourself, it will inevitably have an impact on others in your life and your capacity to enjoy them and their relationships with you.

Chapter 19

On "Be Spontaneous" Paradoxes and Feelings

In our work with couples we encounter many different issues and relationship patterns. However, one of the most interesting dilemmas is what in the professional literature is called the *be spontaneous* paradox. Stated very briefly, a *be spontaneous* paradox is a request for a behavior by the self or another to do something that cannot be done in the way prescribed if requested; or, if requested, it does not meet the conditions of the request in that it is acceptable only if performed without requesting it. That is, it is a request for a behavior that is not subject to conscious control and is therefore one form of a double-bind. You or the other person involved experiences the request as a "damned if I do and damned if I don't" dilemma. For the requester it is a dilemma of "how do I get what I want if I don't ask?" This explanation may sound complicated and perhaps it is. We social scientists have a way of taking something very simple and complicating it. Let's see if we can take off our social scientist hats and communicate it more precisely. Below we provide you with a few examples of some be spontaneous paradoxes in which we frequently find couples enmeshed.

She: "*I want you to tell me you love me.*"
He: "*I love you.*"
She: "*But I had to ask.*"

In this example, the request is made, but the performance of the behavior is not sufficient. It had to be done without asking. This, of course, cannot be done because the request has already been made. Here's another example involving a request for a behavior, but it is only to be performed for the "right" reasons.

She: "*I want you to want to help me with the dishes.*"

He: (Thinking to himself regarding the request.) "I can help Jane with the dishes, but the problem is not that she wants help with the dishes, it is that she wants me to want to help her with the dishes. I can help, but I don't want to. If I do it without wanting to, then I am not responding to her request. I cannot help with the dishes because I don't want to, but I suspect she does want help. On the other hand, if I give the impression of wanting to, then I can be faulted for not doing so sincerely."

In the following example we shift from the interpersonal to the intrapersonal.

"*I wish I wouldn't worry so much. I've got to try harder not to worry, and to feel better.*"

In this intrapersonal dilemma the person berates him/herself for "worrying" and for not feeling good. It is also interesting to note that the roots of this intrapersonal dilemma may well be interpersonal if other people have been telling the person "not to worry" for a long time.

The be spontaneous paradox is, perhaps, the most insidious of personal and interpersonal dilemmas. There is no way to satisfy your requests of yourself and others when posed in a way that constitute what is called a "double-bind" or "damned if I do and damned if I don't" dilemma.

However, we come by the dilemma honestly. As we were growing up, many of us learned from teachers, parents, and others that there are two kinds of feelings: the good feelings, which are okay to have (love, joy, happiness, gratitude, etc.) and the bad feelings, which are not good to have (anger, hate, jealousy, worry, sadness, anxiety, etc.). So we did the logical thing as we learned to *try* to feel the "good" feelings and not to feel the "bad" feelings.

We describe the dilemma and our solutions in the following rules about feelings:

1. There are no good and bad feelings. There are just feelings. We need all of our feelings. All are a part of the human experience. Good and bad feelings are logical complements. You must feel both or you will feel neither. Thus,

    Frustration stands as a logical complement to satisfaction.

    Anxiety is closely tied in meaning to hope.

    Sadness is a complement to joy.

2. Whatever you or others are feeling, it is appropriate for you/them to feel as you/they do given your/their experience and interpretation of the experience. As you and others interpret events differently, so you will each have different feelings about the same events. Very often, we try to "assist" people in interpreting events and thus feeling the way we do—"there is nothing to be afraid of," "there is no reason to worry," "you don't hate your sister," "you're not afraid of Grandpa."

3. By not respecting the validity of your own and others' personal experiences, you pose a be spontaneous paradox for yourself and others. This implies that feelings are subject to conscious control, i.e., that you can through conscious effort will your feelings in and out of you. This is rather like "trying to go to sleep." The harder you try the more awake you become. Similarly, trying "not to worry," "not to be afraid," and "not to be upset" and thus making a conscious effort to get rid of your "bad" feelings (which you are not supposed to have) is doomed to failure. Moreover, such efforts create higher order problems in that you may now feel bad for not being able to get rid of the "bad" feelings. Thus you may feel angry, frustrated, and even depressed for not doing what you are "supposed to"—i.e., get rid of your "bad" feelings. However, now you feel these feelings at a higher level. Of course, this makes you feel even worse. Stated differently, your level one feelings are never a problem if your level two feelings say they are okay. Level two feelings are feelings about your feelings, and the implicit message for you in this essay is that it is okay to feel what you do at level one.

4. While your feelings are not subject to conscious control and you have no choice except to feel what you feel, you have a choice about what you do with those feelings. Your behavior is subject to your and others' conscious control. In other words, you can feel anger, frustration, worry,

joy, love, or hope and choose action alternatives in which these feelings are not exhibited. For example:

You don't have to "want to" to go to work in the morning. You just have to go.

You don't have to "like" changing diapers. You do have to change them.

You don't have to "enjoy" having the neighbors over. You just have to be sociable.

We would like to give you permission to feel what you feel and yet do what you need to do. We give you our permission to worry, to be frustrated, to be angry, to be happy, or to be amused, even when others may not feel as you do. Similarly, we ask that you give others permission to feel what they feel and yet do what needs to be done. For example:

"You don't have to like it. Crab about it all the way, but please take out the trash."

"I know you don't enjoy visiting my parents. That's okay with me, all you need to do is go."

"I don't expect you to like it, all you need to do is do it."

Now it is time for a couple of exercises that may help you free yourself and others to feel what they are feeling.

Exercise 1

First a focus on you. For the next few days, be alert to your feelings—joy, frustration, fulfillment, anger, love, etc. Be especially alert to your feelings about your feelings, such as, "I shouldn't worry, be upset, be angry," etc. When you feel the so-called "bad" feelings, try giving yourself permission to feel what you are feeling—"I'm worried, frustrated, angry, etc., and that's the way it is." Feel the freedom to feel what you do. "For me, in this circumstance, given my interpretation of events, whatever I feel makes sense and is appropriate."

Exercise 2

Now a focus on others. This may be harder, for we often go to great lengths to get people to be more pleasant to be around. However, we ask you to give them permission to feel as they do. It is right and appropriate to feel as they do in their circumstances and given their interpretation of events. You are not in their shoes, and it is not fair to tell them what their experience should be. It may be a different experience from yours, but yours is not the "right" experience. "I know you don't want to and that is okay, all you need to do is do the dishes." "I know it is a real pain to get up in the middle of the night, and I don't want to ask, but I need a full night's sleep.

All of your feelings are a part of who you are. Very often we mean well when we try to help ourselves and others get rid of the "bad" feelings and replace them with "good" feelings. However, often we experience this "help" as a message that we are lovable only when we feel the "good" feelings. It has been said that love is time and space measured by the heart. Similarly, love is not contingent upon feeling only the right feelings at the right time to suit others. Thus, love may also be acceptance of our own and others' feelings measured by the heart.

Chapter 20

Getting Out of the Box

In another essay we left you hanging in suspense for the solution to the nine-dot problem. But if by chance you haven't read that essay, we will bring you up to date. We presented the puzzle illustrated below with instructions to connect all nine dots with four straight lines without lifting your pencil from the paper. Try it now. (We have provided you with a couple of opportunities to find the solution.)

For many people first attempts to solve the problem bog down in frustration. The problem lies in the assumption that the nine dots form a square and that the solution must be found by staying within the boundaries of the square. However, the instructions did not (1) define the nine dots as a square, nor (2) impose a rule that the solutions must be found by staying within the "square." The puzzle is readily solvable, but only if you give up the self-imposed assumptions that the rules do not contain. Indeed, no such boundary exists. The solution to the puzzle may be found at the end of this essay.

As you can see, once we give up the assumption that the nine dots define a square, we are free to consider alternatives and creative solutions. In this instance, it freed us to go beyond the square. From within the square no solution to the puzzle is possible. As we examine and set aside our assumption of squareness, a solution becomes not only possible but seems exceedingly simple.

"Hmm. That's pretty clever, but what's the point?" you might ask. Well, we're glad you asked, because we do have a point. The point is that there are many different perspectives or interpretations for any given event. Each interpretation provides us with a logical course of action consistent with that interpretation. In other words, each person's actions will make sense to him/her given the way that person interprets the events or makes assumptions about them. If the person had a different interpretation, she/he would take a different course of action. We hope that the nine-dot puzzle illustrates how we can get caught in a box, or in a specific way of interpreting events and in following courses of action consistent with our interpretation as we attempt to solve problems. The good news is that as we come up with different interpretations, different possible solutions become available for problems that previously seemed unsolvable. The sequence within us might be described as follows:

1. Event occurs.

2. Meaning is experienced.

3. Effect or feelings are experienced consistent with the meaning.

4. Action is taken consistent with meaning and action.

As the event is given a different meaning, different feelings and different action alternatives emerge.

"Aha, that makes sense," you say, but then you ask, "But what is the real explanation or interpretation?"

"That's a good question," we respond. "We don't know and we don't believe the real explanation or interpretation is available to us as finite beings who don't have a God's eye view of the world. There are no immaculate perceptions. All of our interpretations are possibly true and they are also possibly distortions of a reality that we cannot know."

So where does this leave you? It leaves you to live with an element of uncertainty and a great deal of freedom as you live your life and create your reality. Perhaps you will search for the best possible interpretation of events and, acting on this interpretation, will observe whether the desired results occur. Thus you become a scientist who engages in experiments in living. If the desired results do not occur, perhaps you will examine your assumptions or your interpretation of events, consider an alternative interpretation that suggests an alternative course of action, and again observe the results. You seek to validate the theory, interpretation, or explanation that works for you in your particular circumstances.

We'll give you a couple of examples to illustrate our point:

Harry and Martha have been married for 20 years. The children are grown and away at school and/or are on their own, more or less. For 20 years, Harry has been the sole bread winner and Martha has been the keeper of the home and hearth. Martha announces that she would like to get a job. Harry could interpret this announcement as (a) Martha making a comment about him and his ability to support the family. In this case, it would be logical for him to fight it, defend himself, and try to talk her out of it; or (b) Martha needing new challenges and opportunities for her many talents and a desire to redirect her restless energy. In this case, he could support, encourage, and be excited for her. The interpretation of the event is very important; it can solve a problem or it can create a problem.

Harriet and Peter have been married for three years and have just had their first child. This is potentially both the most blessed and yet the most disruptive event that could occur in terms of the routine of their relationship. Harriet and Peter have less private time together. Harriet is preoccupied with the child and directs less energy toward Peter. She is tired more frequently. Peter could interpret the events as (a) Harriet's caring for him less, and he could withdraw, become upset, and gripe about how she doesn't have time for him; or (b) a necessary period of adjustment required to evolve a new set of routines in the family. In this case, he could provide support and pitch in by doing things he did not do previously so that he and Harriet can have more time together.

In each example above, both (a) and (b) are plausible explanations. Many other interpretations are also possible, and neither (a) nor (b) is true in an absolute sense. However, it is our belief that the (b) interpretations are more useful toward evolving a satisfactory marriage/relationship or family.

Let's move now to an exercise that may help you examine your assumptions and your interpretation of events in your marriage/relationship and your family.

Exercise 1

This is an exercise for the two of you to do individually. Over the next few weeks, we ask that you be alert to your feelings, particularly those feelings that you don't like to have—anger, frustration, hurt, etc. Remember that your feelings are closely tied to your interpretation of events, which, in turn, moves you to a specific course of action to help you get rid of the feeling you do not want. When you have one of these feelings, we ask you to pause for a few moments (if possible) and to ask yourself the following questions:

1. How am I interpreting this situation?

2. What assumptions am I making?

3. If I follow the logic of these assumptions, what actions make sense?

4. What alternative interpretations are plausible?

5. What logical courses of action make sense if I assume the alternative interpretations to be true?

We do not really expect you to take the few moments for reflection each time you feel one of the feelings that are not fun to have. Very probably you will respond as you usually do in the moment of crisis. However, even though you have taken action in the moment, perhaps later when your feelings have been tempered somewhat, the moments of reflection may provide you with alternatives to your course of action should the same situation arise again.

We wish you well as you begin to see the boxes you are in and begin to play with the possible ways to get out of them. However, as always, please be patient with yourself and don't expect miracles. Change is always a challenging process.

THE SOLUTION TO THE NINE-DOT PROBLEM

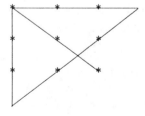

Chapter 21

Shame and Guilt in Relationships

M any of us have a fear of being criticized, especially by our spouses/part-ners or others whom we love. As the recipients of criticism we feel as though we are unlovable, that we have somehow failed, or that we are worthless. However, criticism is not necessarily a bad thing. Nor is it necessarily good. Even so-called "constructive criticism" can have a negative impact. For it is not what is said (the content), it is how it is said (the process) that is important when communicating criticism. Especially in a loving relationship, it is crucial that the process be one of guilting rather than one of shaming.

When we guilt someone, we criticize a behavior but not the person. When we shame someone, we devalue the whole person. Further, guilting acknow-ledges a sense of relationship. That is, we are in this together, I care about you, and what you do affects me. Shaming, on the other hand, denies the fact of a relationship and of mutual responsibility. There is an attempt to place respon-sibility or blame entirely on the other and this automatically denies a caring concern for that person.

For example, Anne has worked very hard all day to prepare a special dinner for Mike. Before he left for work she specifically asked that Mike be home on time for dinner. Mike, however, got hung up at the office with a last minute client. He did not call Anne to let her know he would be late, and when he walks in she is justifiably angry. How Anne communicates her anger will have important ramifications not only for the rest of the evening but for the future of their relationship. If Anne chooses a guilting response to Mike's behavior, she may say something like the following:

"I feel very frustrated by your lack of consideration. I worked very hard to do something nice for us, and you didn't even bother to come home on time. I'm afraid our special dinner is ruined."

If she chooses a shaming response, she may say:

"You are so inconsiderate. You never do anything I ask you."

In the first response, Anne communicates both how she is feeling and how Mike's behavior has affected her and her plans for the two of them. Clearly, Mike, their relationship, and how Mike's behavior influences the relationship is important to her. In the second response, Anne just blames Mike and does not communicate anything about how she is feeling or why. Obviously, while Mike has indeed been inconsiderate, Anne's behavior does not bode well for their relationship either. However, even in the first response, there is an important piece missing. We call this piece feedforward.

While it is certainly legitimate to criticize the behavior of another in a caring way, we feel it is only fair to also request the behavior that you would consider more appropriate in the future, or feedforward. Otherwise, while you have let the other person know what you don't like, you haven't told them what you would like. Ideally, Anne's response to Mike would be something like the following:

"I feel very frustrated by your lack of consideration. I worked very hard to do something special for us, and you didn't even bother to come home on time. I'm afraid our special dinner is ruined. In the future, I would really appreciate a phone call the moment you know there is a chance that you are going to be late. I realize that this may inconvenience you and I'm sorry, but it would mean a great deal to me."

With this kind of response Anne has given Mike a clear picture of what she believes he did wrong in a way that does not demean him as a person. Anne has also been clear about how Mike could meet her expectations in the future. She has provided a guilt-based message coupled with feedforward. Now we invite you to try the following exercise in order to experience what we have been talking about. As usual, we hope you will do it during a private, quiet time without interruptions or intrusions. Remember, soft music and candlelight can make even the most tedious exercises more pleasant ("A spoonful of sugar helps the medicine go down...").

Exercise 1

Each of you takes a few minutes to think of a minor annoyance in the other's behavior. Then take turns expressing how you feel when your spouse/partner does _____ and the impact you feel this has on your relationship. Then tell your spouse/partner the specific behavior you would prefer him or her to do in the future. Before reversing roles, thank your spouse/partner for caring enough to let you know both what she/he doesn't like and what she/he would like. Neither of you should make any grand promises about what you will do in the future. The most you can offer is to try to change, knowing that you may not always be successful. After you have both had a turn, give each other a hug and do something fun together.

We have no illusions about the difficulty of incorporating this kind of behavior into your communication repertoire. But we also know the payoffs can be significant. Guilt-based responses send a message of care and concern. Feedforward adds a dimension of fairness that we think everyone would like to experience in their relationships.

Chapter 22

Family Traditions

We often become keenly aware of our need for stability when we are confronted with change and difference. For example, while moving from one city to another may be an adventure, it is also a challenge as the old and familiar disappear from our lives. Saying goodbye to friends, finishing projects, creating a new home, and beginning work and social relationships in a different setting suddenly become a part of the daily routine. The unfamiliar is now a constant companion. However, the stress of the unfamiliar may be alleviated to a degree if we bring our family traditions with us. Such routines and rituals are a great comfort even in quiet times. But in times of upheaval and uncertainty they become the necessary balance for change, a source of stability in otherwise unpredictable and unsettling circumstances.

The family traditions of which we tend to be most aware are those of the various holiday seasons. Decorating homes, planning celebrations, preparing special foods are all parts of patterns that we brought with us from our families of origin and adapted to fit new relationships and families. Equally important, however, are those less obvious habits we have created to help define our particular relationship/family and make it unique. Indeed, whether they are part of festival occasions or daily routines, the observance of rituals and traditions has been found to be an important characteristic of healthy families. Rituals tend to enhance group identity and allow members to accept growth, change, and loss while maintaining a basic sense of continuity.

In the following exercises, we invite you to consider and evaluate your family traditions. We also challenge you to enhance those which are positive, eliminate those which are negative, and create new ones where none presently exist. As usual, we suggest that these exercises be done by couples during a time and a place where both privacy and comfort are possible.

Exercise 1

Make a list of all the holidays and special occasions you typically observe during the year. Your list would probably include such things as birthdays, Halloween, Thanksgiving, Christmas, Hanukkah and/or other religious holidays, Valentine's Day, Mother's Day, Father's Day, etc. Share with each other how these events were celebrated in your families of origin. Then reflect on the process involved in creating traditions around each of these events in your own family. Did they just happen or did you plan how you wanted them to be? Are there things that you would like to change? If you plan to make changes, how can you let the rest of the family in on these plans?

Exercise 2

Make a list of all the little routines and habits in which you typically engage each day of your lives together. Your list might include bedtime routines, the way in which you start your day, the way you greet each other when you come into the house, mealtime rituals, the way announcements are made, the way disagreements are handled, etc. Probably some of these traditions are more positive than others, but they are all part of who you are as a family. Do your "family traditions" say what you want them to say about your relationship and about your family? Are there some pieces that you would like to add or subtract? How can you make this happen?

Family traditions acknowledge both tangible and intangible realities. Part of their power lies in their ability to foster family identity. They are part of the heritage that was provided for us by our parents and that we in turn provide for ourselves and our children. They help us to know who we are even in the midst of turmoil and confusion. We therefore feel they are worthy of conscious consideration and creation. For, as we celebrate in both large and small ways, we are able not only to maintain continuity with the past but to move forward optimistically into the future.

Chapter 23

Grouch

As you read not only ours but other essays about how to have a successful marriage/relationship, you might get the impression that you always must keep smiling and be cheerful at best, and at worst you always must rationally and logically work through your differences. But sometimes things do not work out this way. Sometimes you may not feel like responding as asked when someone says "Smile," "Cheer up," or "Don't you know it's wonderful just to be alive?" Sometimes it is not only important, but necessary to have a good grouch.

We do get sick and tired of everything from time to time and a healthy impulse may be to shuck the many ways we are "supposed to be" and to put on a good grouch. Indeed, sometimes we get sick and tired of everything except being sick and tired of it all. However, it seems that our society has greater tolerance for anyone else than for one who is sick and tired of it all.

If we can tolerate all the "shoulds" and "supposed to be's" that designers for our lives impose upon us, why can't we tolerate a person who desires only a one-hour, a one-day, or a three-day respite from the smiles? Inside we may be seething and looking for a context where we can break out of it, where we can engage in our grouch without the inevitable concern for our welfare, well-being, and without the predictable "cheer-up!" or "smile."

On the other hand, it may be enjoyable to have our grouch with other people around. They will undoubtedly become counselors. And to their "cheer up" we can respond, "Why should I?" Of course, these people will try to solve our "problem(s)." We suspect, however, that they are just envious of us and wish they could give themselves permission to be grouchy. Sometimes we just don't want to "win friends and influence people." We would rather experience clean, clear air devoid of social protocol and niceties.

It is a strange thing about grouchiness. It seems to be okayer as one gets older. Children often refer to older people as "old grouches." Maybe grouchiness comes with wisdom, with a perspective on life and many of the absurdities we have been living with so seriously. At the other end of the spectrum are the children who are being taught appropriate behavior. They are not allowed to be grouchy at all, and if they are, they are likely to be sent to their room or even for a psychological evaluation.

From time to time parents may feel free to be grouchy with each other and more often with their children. But the rules of society demand that despite our grouchy mood and behavior with each other, we must shift to our cheery voice when answering the phone or meeting someone who is not a member of our family. We do not seem to have permission to be grouchy in public.

Grouchiness binges, however, are important to our sanity, and they are important to people of all ages. Age is no barrier to being sick and tired of it all. (Of course, to be grouchy all of the time deprives one of the pleasure of the respite from social roles, rules, and regulations that grouchiness binges afford us.) Nevertheless, how often and how long your grouchiness binges should be is a rather personal decision. We find it useful to engage in a grouchiness binge just before we get hooked into grouchiness by the natural flow of events, just before we are inclined to shout, "I'm sick and tired of it all!"

Of course, if you exercise your right to have a grouchy hour or day, you must realize that others in your world must have the same right. We emphasize the importance of this reciprocal right. It is just not fair for you to exercise your right to be grouchy and to deny your spouse/partner or children this same right.

It is only fair to announce to others that you are going to be grouchy and that while they may approach you, they do so at their own risk. Giving fair warning allows them to be ready. On the other hand, sometimes grouchiness sneaks up on us, and we may exercise our right to be grouchy when we may not have the inclination or the opportunity to warn others. This is important too, and your spouse/partner and children may need to give you the appropriate distance, knowing that you are just exercising your right to be grouchy and it is not personal to them. Let's call this the spontaneous grouch privilege.

There is another dimension to this right to grouch, which we alluded to above. If you are feeling grouchy regarding something specific the other person did to you and you decide to be grouchy, then this is not a legitimate, general grouch. This is a punitive, personal grouch and is not really fair to others. The general grouch is okay and can even be fun for everyone. On the other hand, the punitive, personal grouch doesn't really help very much and may turn into a mind-reading, "What have I done now?" exercise. This can evolve into a reciprocal punitive, personal grouch at you for your grouchiness for not specifying at whom and about what you are grouchy. If someone offended you in some way, that person deserves to know just what it is that has upset you. And you need to have this same privilege.

We have stated our case regarding the merits and limits of grouchiness. Should you exercise your right and privilege to be grouchy? This, as we said, is a personal decision. As noted previously, different people will need varying amounts of time for their grouch. You might legitimately ask, "What if everyone in the family decided to go on a grouch at the same time?" Our response: "It might be fun!" To reiterate, there are decided limits to being smiley and cheery all of the time. Some days things just don't go the way they are supposed to go. It happens to us, and we know it happens to you. The right to be grouchy is a part of our personal survival kits. We hope it will also be useful to you.

Should you decide to try it out, we suggest that you begin by giving those persons around whom you will be grouchy a copy of this essay. At least they will understand what you are doing. And perhaps they might decide to try it themselves. In another essay we recommend that you *"Live your life so that if you go crazy, people will not know the difference."* In closing this essay we suggest that you allow grouchiness to become a part of your craziness. Why should the privilege belong only to the very old? Why not have a child grouch, a young adult grouch, and a middle-aged grouch, as well as the "old grouch?"

Chapter 24

Learning To Be Crazy

In our work as teachers of marriage and family therapy/studies, one of the most important concepts we seek to impart to our students is the notion that in any relationship a stable, predictable pattern of behavior evolves in a relatively short time. This redundant pattern comprises the implicit contract about how the two people in the relationship have agreed to be and to do with each other. People in a relationship pretty quickly establish how they will interact with each other and tend to keep doing the same things in the same or similar kinds of situations. This is not good or bad, it just is.

This redundant pattern, for good or ill, becomes the basis both for the identity of each person in the relationship and for the identity of the relationship as a whole. Indeed, we need the stability/predictability/constancy of our relationships and their redundant patterns in order to maintain our sense of who we are, who the other is, and who we are together. Further, in each of our relationships we have a somewhat different experience of who we are.

While this stability is important, in a functional relationship both stability and change are essential. It is a fundamental paradox that stability in a relationship is maintained by change and that when a relationship is appropriately stable, it can change. We need our redundant/stable/predictable relationships as well as difference/variety/excitement. The dilemma is that while redundancy and routine seem to emerge without conscious effort, difference, variety, and excitement tend to take plotting and conscious effort. However, this is effort that energizes.

We invite you now to engage in an experiment to illustrate the concept of redundancy/stability/predictability in a relationship, as well as the impact of changing, or being a little bit crazy.

Exercise 1

In your family or in your relationship with your spouse/partner, do something "different." We define as "different" anything that is out of the ordinary for the usual way you are/do in a particular relationship. Some of the different things you might do include the following: enter the house differently, perhaps whistling, singing, and/or skipping; greet your spouse/partner differently, perhaps with an amorous hug rather than the usual "hello" as you reach for the newspaper or turn on the television; get into bed differently, perhaps from the wrong side so you have to roll over your spouse/partner; serve dinner in the dining room with cloth napkins; light and place a candle on the breakfast table; sit at a different place for meals. Other things you might do include: put the sugar bowl in the refrigerator; hang a picture upside-down; insist on doing the dishes; stick balloons on walls throughout the house; blow bubbles; place a cartoon on the back of the toilet seat. The number of different things you can do is limited only by your imagination. As you plot and do the different things in your experiment, you may feel a bit like a child, perhaps a little excited, perhaps a bit anxious. That's okay! That's how you are supposed to feel!

Exercise 2

When you have done your first "different" thing, watch and listen to the reaction of your spouse/partner and/or children. Typical reactions you might expect include "What's wrong?" "What's with you?" "Are you all right?" His or her eyes may roll a bit or she/he may look puzzled and give a shake of the head. No matter what his/her response, don't explain. Simply say, "I just felt like it," or "It seemed like a good idea." If push comes to shove, you can always blame us for making the suggestion.

We leave you with a last thought that we rather like and seek to live in our relationship with each other as well as with the members of our family: *Live your life so that if you go crazy, people will not know the difference!*

Chapter 25

Lessons from Childhood

As teachers we have to be good researchers who are involved in the creation and dissemination of knowledge. But as teachers we must also be good borrowers. Thus we read widely and on diverse topics, and occasionally we find an idea in a different discipline that is useful in our primary areas of interest—marriage and the family. When this occurs, a part of our task is to build bridges between seemingly unrelated disciplines. In a sense, the ideas or concepts are not ours and yet, in another sense the new concept is very much our own, since we have found a connection that others may not have seen. Such connections more closely resemble what we call "wisdom" rather than "knowledge."

In this essay we build on what to us is a magnificently simple concept with far-reaching implications. Very often such simple ideas become wonderful tools when we use our basic talents for reflection. Some time ago, Robert Fulghum published a short, one-page article entitled "All I Ever Needed to Know I Learned in Kindergarten" in the magazine *Church and Public Education*. Eventually this article was expanded to a small book and even appears today on posters.

To fully appreciate the wisdom of Fulghum's message, we ask you to go back a few, or perhaps many, years to your first experience in school. For some of you it was nursery school or kindergarten. Those of you who are older may have had your first school experience in first grade. But wherever you began, we venture to guess that you can recall some of the things that Fulghum recounts from his experience. Sit back and listen to what he learned, read it aloud and thoughtfully:

Share everything, play fair, don't hit people. Put things back where you found them. Clean up your own mess. Don't take things that aren't yours. Say you're sorry when you hurt somebody. Wash your hands before you eat. Flush. Warm cookies and cold milk are good for you. Live a balanced life. Learn some and think some and draw and paint and play and work every day some. Take a nap every afternoon. When you go out into the world, watch for traffic, hold hands and stick together. Be aware of wonder. Goldfish and hamsters and white mice and even the little seed in the plastic cup—they all die. So do we. And then remember the book about Dick and Jane and the first word you learned, the biggest word of all: LOOK. Everything you need to know is in there somewhere. The Golden Rule and love and basic sanitation, Ecology and politics and sane living.

We'll let you add your own memories of what you learned in those simpler, perhaps more secure, days before becoming grown-ups.

Occasionally we feel harried, hurried, and overwhelmed with the seeming complexity of today's world. Is it really so complex, or have we misplaced our priorities and had our minds muddied by hair-splitting rules for living that overcomplicate our lives? We do not suggest that your life as an adult is not different than it was as a child. We simply ask you to reflect on Fulghum's and our simple idea and let your own wisdom evolve about what is important for you and for those you love.

Chapter 26

Addition, Not Subtraction: Let Us Not Cease from Dreaming

In the process of helping couples as they struggle to make their relationships better, a phenomenon we frequently observe is their repeated and often futile attempts to subtract or get rid of problems. In this mode couples view problems as "active agents that need to be attacked" and thus may spend a large percentage of their relationship time "attacking." Indeed, we sometimes wonder whether they would even have a relationship if there were no problems to be attacked. And when couples come for consultation or therapy, we may be asked to join them in their resolve to eliminate their differences or solve some of their problems. While this can be a useful activity, sometimes it is important to move them to a different focus.

In this spirit, we are reminded of the story of the city feller who asked the farmer for directions to town. After pondering the question for some time, the farmer turned to the city feller and said, "I know where you want to go, but you can't get there from here." Similarly, many couples cannot get where they say they would like to go from where they are and by means of the process they are using to get there.

On the other hand, some couples don't know where they want to go. They are very specific about the problems they have in their relationship, but they have only vague ideas about their destination or how they would like things to be. We often describe these couples as people making very sincere efforts to get to an unspecified place through means that keep them in the same place. While helping them solve some problems may be our focus, an additional focus is to assist them in developing very specific images of where they would like to be and what they would be doing with each other if things were better. An additional part of this process is to consider the "addition function," or what parts of their image of how they would like to be can they begin to do now. In essence, we seek to help them begin to live pieces of their dream as an adjunct to or in place of their problem-solving activities.

There will always be differences and problems to solve. No two people in a relationship solve all problems for all time, ever. However, this reality does not necessarily have to diminish the other aspects of the relationship that can be lived in addition to problem-solving. To us, resolving differences and solving problems represent subtraction. Learning to live a bit of one's dreams and enjoying one another is a function of addition. With these thoughts in mind, we present two activities you may find useful.

Exercise 1

Find a time when the two of you can be together for about an hour. Again, take the phone off the hook and give yourselves some privacy from the children. Let's call this dream time. Together, brainstorm your dreams and ideal visions about your lives together and the exact form these would take in daily living. No holds barred. A dream is not limited to what is possible, so there is to be no reality testing by either of you. This activity may include designing your dream house or dreaming of things like taking time to go fishing or hiking together, a dinner with just the two of you, private time to just read together, back rubs, or surprising each other with something special. It can also include private dreams for each of you: going back to school, writing a book, getting a job, exercising, or backpacking into a wilderness area. Indeed, private dreams are as important as shared dreams, and in our vision spouses/partners can support each other's efforts to pursue private dreams.

Exercise 2

Without comment, discussion, or commitment about what each of you will do, slowly begin to implement incremental pieces of your dream. A dream becomes reality through the act of beginning to live it in small ways. It may be as simple as feeding the children alone and preparing a meal just for the two of you after the children have gone to bed. It may begin with investigating courses you might take at a local school. It may begin by purchasing a subscription to a magazine that is of special interest to you or your spouse/partner.

The addition function may not make all problems go away, but a strange thing about implementing pieces of a dream is that putting something in forces something out. Again and again throughout this collection of essays we have attempted to emphasize the following ideas:

Principle I: A happy marriage or family is one in which its members make happy things happen.

Corollary: May your spouse or other family members become paranoid that you or other family members are plotting to help them be happy.

Chapter 27

But Let There Be Spaces in Your Togetherness

The title of this essay comes from *The Prophet* by Kahlil Gibran. In this beautiful volume, which is a collection of perspectives on life, living, and loving, we find the following advice regarding marriage:

> Sing and dance together and be joyous,
>   but let each one of you be alone
> Even as the strings of a lute are alone
>   though they quiver with the same music.
> And stand together yet not too near together;
> For the pillars of the temple stand apart,
> And the oak tree and the cypress grow
>   not in each other's shadow.
> But let there be spaces in your togetherness
> And let the winds of the heavens dance between you.

In many ways Gibran's words speak for themselves and thus we offer but a few brief comments on them. First we wish to point out a fundamental paradox in interpersonal relationships: people will tend to attempt to individuate or separate themselves where there is pressure to conform, and people will choose to participate in or conform to the relationship or system when there is freedom to individuate.

We are also reminded that marriage or other couple relationships should not cost either partner his/her personal identity or his/her personal space. Further, as each partner in a relationship assists the other to maintain his/her personal identity and space, to that degree is the relationship valued and enhanced, paradoxically facilitating togetherness.

We may depict the paradox as follows:

1. Attempts to produce this ....

    lead to this ....

2. Freedom and assistance to produce this ....

    lead to this ....

We invite you to do the following:

Exercise 1

Plan a time to be together when you can do so without interruptions from children, telephone, television, etc. Turn on your favorite music, share your favorite beverage, and tune out the world for a while. First, consider the need that each of you has for space, both emotional and physical. Is one of you more outgoing, more social in terms of a desire to get together with other people? Does one of you need time to retreat and recuperate periodically from the daily hubbub? Does one of you like to think things over before responding while the other prefers instant discussion and decision-making? How do you respect these differences in style? Are there requests that you would like to make to accommodate such differences?

Exercise 2

Do a mental search of your home, considering where each of you can go to be alone. Do you each have a space you can call your own? We feel it is extremely important for each member of a couple to have a place to go where a closed door or a "do not disturb" sign will be respected. If possible, these should be separate spaces where each can put his/her own things. Can you think of ways to make this happen in your home?

An important thing to remember is that one person's need for alone time is not a rejection of the other person. Further, one chooses the time to retreat carefully so that it is not perceived as a rejection. Perhaps you might consider saying something like, "I love you very much, but I just need to be alone for a while." And remember, as one person takes space for him/herself, the other person is given space. As we said above, paradoxically, togetherness thus becomes more meaningful.

But let there be spaces in your togetherness
And let the winds of the heavens dance between you.

Chapter 28

How Shall We Create Our Relationship? Let Me Count the Ways

The title of this essay is a variation of the first line of the sonnet by Elizabeth Barrett Browning that begins, "How Do I Love thee, Let me count the ways." Indeed, there are many ways that one may love another. Similarly, a successful marriage/relationship necessarily involves many ways of being together.

As two people enter a relationship, each pragmatically asks, "How shall we be with each other to our individual and mutual satisfaction?" But they must also remember that how they are to be with each other must shift and evolve to fit changing circumstances in their lives. Couples can speak of their first, second, third, and fourth marriages/relationships with the same spouse/partner. While there is continuity to life, there are also changes that must be made to accommodate changing circumstances. Salvador Minuchin noted that, "Each new scenario is an experiment in living." To us this statement is a powerful reminder that life and living together necessitate many adjustments and experiments about how to live when you are faced with both expected and unexpected challenges.

In today's world many people are married or involved in committed relationships more than once. Perhaps they search for a different way to be together, a way that fits their definition of a successful marriage/relationship. Very often transitions from one marriage/relationship to another are made at crisis points that stress and challenge the way the couple has been together up to that time. When a couple does not evolve a different way to be together to fit the changes or challenges in their lives, an end to the relationship can be the result. However, crisis points or normal life transitions are inevitable, and appropriate adaptation promotes continuity and stability.

Researchers have identified several crisis points in the life of a family. Some of both the expected and the unexpected challenges requiring adaption and change include the following:

EXPECTED CHALLENGES

- The addition of a child
- Children going to school and engaging in more activities
- Adolescence of children
- Children leaving home
- Retirement
- Aging parents

UNEXPECTED CHALLENGES

- Winning a large amount of money
- Death of a family member
- Sickness of a family member
- Unemployment of the major breadwinner
- A grandparent coming to live with the family
- Family member going off to war

Certainly there are many more challenges that require adaptation and adjustment. Perhaps you can identify a few challenges that required shifts in your roles as spouses/partners that are not included in the above lists. For example, consider the following situations that required major transformation:

John and Harriet had been together for twenty years. Their three children were in adolescence. John had been employed in the same position for seventeen years, and Harriet had been working part-time for two years, having begun when the youngest child was twelve. This couple's vision of the future was not exciting, but it was comfortable for both. However, a major economic recession quickly changed the picture. John's job was phased out in a corporate reorganization, and the limited number of opportunities in their area made alternate employment impossible. Out of necessity, Harriet moved from part-time to full-time employment, and she took advantage of whatever overtime opportunities were available. Major role changes were obviously necessitated. John took over the housekeeping and parenting roles formerly performed by Harriet, who was now the major breadwinner. The children had to adjust to John's style. John, a hard-working male who had been reared in a traditional family, grieved the loss of his identity and did not take easily to the changes. Harriet, reared in a similar kind of family, was upset by her inability to spend more time with her children. There was tension as all family members were forced to adapt in order to assure continuity of the family.

Peter and Joan lived a very comfortable dual-career lifestyle for the first four years of their relationship. They enjoyed a routine that allowed them great latitude of movement and a variety of activities with little advanced preparation. They eagerly anticipated the birth of their first child, and it was a joyous occasion when Henry was born. What they had not fully anticipated was the shift in roles that was required as they worked to accommodate Henry's needs. Peter continued to work his regular job, but Joan reduced her job to a part-time status. The amount of available money dropped off, and the expenses increased. Ease and spontaneity of movement became more complicated, and both Peter and Joan felt the increased demands on their time. Their first relationship was over, and their second had begun, requiring the creation of a new way to be together with Henry as a part of the family and their lives.

We suspect you are getting our point by now, but let's look at one more:

At age 65 Paul retired. Lorraine, who had been a full-time housewife and mother with clear, free days ever since the children left home, was now faced with having Paul around the house for twenty-four hours a day instead of the usual twelve hours plus weekends. Paul suddenly had all the time he used to spend at work on his hands and didn't know what to do with himself.

He also did not know what to do with Lorraine for twenty-four hours a day. The way Paul and Lorraine renegotiate their relationship with each other will greatly influence their experience of retirement.

The situations described above focus on three major transitions in the life of a family. However, in the average couple's life together, there are also many mini-transitions that require adaption and adjustment, such as changing from the day shift to the evening shift, joining a club, going back to school, or taking up jogging. You cannot do just one thing. Each movement by one affects the other.

Relationship discussions anticipating the necessary adjustments relative to both mini and major transitions may help lessen the stress of these events. At the same time, it is important to remember that the best-designed plans must be lived out. Further, any change in how each of you is with the other breaks old patterns and routines, so typically the adjustments are emotionally charged.

We have said enough to give you a perspective on the idea that you have been and will be together many different ways over the course of your marriage/relationship. We will now give you the opportunity to reflect on the transitions you may have made during your years together and to perhaps anticipate some of the changes requiring adaptations that you may face in the future.

Exercise 1

Find a quiet place and time away from other people and distractions and spend a short time reliving and reflecting on the different transitions the two of you have experienced in your lives together. Consider the kinds of adaptations you made in response to these transitions, including both those with which you are pleased in retrospect and those which you would do differently if you had them to do over.

Chapter 29

Looking Back and Looking Ahead

There is a real continuity to life as beginnings and endings flow together, ever changing and yet similar. So it is in this final piece in our little collection of essays. Thus we provide closure and at the same time attempt to plant seeds for continuing growth and renewal as we offer a summary of our perspective on successful marriages/relationships and families. As we have said many times, there is no one way a marriage/relationship or a family should be, but research on successful families provides clues that may be potentially useful. It is also important to remind you that our summary does not do justice to the wealth of available literature and that it is filtered through the lenses of our personal biases.

One of the most significant transitions a family experiences occurs when the children leave home, join other systems, and form new relationships as a ritual to prepare themselves for the start of the next generation of families. This leaving home is a happy-sad experience for all involved. However, even as the child leaves home, she/he also brings home with him or her. The family's values, mores, methods of being husband/wife/partner and parents are deeply etched in each child. During his/her growing-up years in the family, the child assumed a role, developed an identity, and acquired those characteristics/behaviors best suited to playing out his/her family role. The child then tends to transfer these role behaviors into relationships outside the family. In effect, the child brings his/her role and his/her conceptions of self and family into the new family.

Thus, while the newly married couple or newly established relationship is often viewed as the beginning of a new family, each spouse/partner will in fact either carry on or react in opposition to the traditions and values brought from his/her family of origin. Some spouses/partners try to replicate their families of origin, while others seek to make their families better in some ways than the families they experienced as they were growing up. But whether or not one tries to make his/her family similar or different, there is loyalty to the experience in one's family of origin.

Indeed, there is some evidence that spouses/partners are initially attracted to each other on the basis of perceived compatibility of roles each brought from the family of origin. The family of origin provides people with their basic ideas about how a family should be, including the unspoken rules that regulate the behavior of all members of a family.

One of the initial tasks of a new couple is to negotiate the spouse/partner roles. For many couples this new twenty-four-hour-a-day exposure brings many surprises that the courtship period did not reveal. This seems to be true even for couples who lived together prior to their marriage or permanent commitment. That is, living together before marriage/commitment only seems to help couples assess how well they can live together before marriage/commitment. Living together after marriage/commitment is decidedly different. Somehow the public affirmation of vows seems to produce both subtle and dramatic changes in the relationship. One might explain the difference as one of moving from choice to no longer having a choice. Our society values the institutions of marriage and the family and thus makes it easier to get into than out of them. This is an important difference.

Even when the families of origin are very similar, spouses/partners face the necessity of adjusting and negotiating their roles relative to each other. They are evolving a new family and yet have great allegiance to their families of origin (this can be in support of or in opposition to). The bonds of rules and roles of the original families are very strong. The new couple may find themselves "playing house" for a while as they adapt and adjust to each other and evolve a relatively stable pattern and predictable structure. As we noted above, there may be many surprises. Both spouses/partners may overtly and/or covertly exert pressure to change the other's behavior and role to "fit," or try to redesign the other to be the way she/he is "supposed to be" so the marriage or family can be the way it is "supposed to be." It does not take long for a stable pattern to emerge, however, and this pattern may be built in the process of attempting to change each other to some conception of the ideal husband/wife/partner.

To illustrate, if one partner's family of origin is "A" and the other's family of origin is "B," then the couple will ultimately need to evolve a "C," their family pattern. "C" will be a blend of "A" and "B," which, in combination, forms a unique configuration. And this unique configuration may include fighting over whether "C" should look more like "A" or "B."

In earlier times (not necessarily better), the process of evolving a new family pattern was perhaps somewhat easier in that the social roles of men and women were fewer and more circumscribed. A woman was X and a man was Y, and the rule was that there should forever be a division of labor and roles. Today's world is more complex because members of each sex have more role options. While this may look extremely attractive, it makes the negotiating process more challenging. Another complication is that these new role conceptions for spouses/partners are ideas, concepts, and ideals. While they are intellectually appealing, few of us were prepared for them emotionally in our families of origin, where a more traditional conception of the husband/wife roles was probably experienced. Thus there is often a conflict between the intellectual ideas about husband/wife/partner roles and one's "gut" reactions. A spouse/partner may be emotionally and naturally predisposed to maintain the pattern of relationships experienced in the family of origin, but through learning and experience in other contexts may see different options as desirable. However, even when both spouses/partners share the ideal of alternate roles as better, the emotional tug is to their early experience. This behavior comes easily, while the alternative roles require constant and conscious effort.

While the struggle to evolve a workable marriage/relationship with complementary roles may not be easy, it is the basis for a good strong partnership, which in turn is the basis for the parental coalition needed if and when children enter the family. The idea of a coalition connotes a sense of "we-ness" between spouses/partners. During courtship, the first budding of this "we-ness" emerged as a deep caring, respect for difference, and sufficient agreement that the couple chose to marry or make a permanent commitment.

Difference and respect for difference are a great source of strength for a marriage/relationship coalition. As we have indicated many times previously, difference is a resource without which one is limited when faced with the varied challenges of life in a family. Accordingly, the fact that she does one thing better than he is respected and utilized. Likewise, the fact that he does another thing better than she is also respected and utilized.

The many demands of evolving roles, handling finances, developing a lifestyle, setting priorities within and without the home, and perhaps rearing children necessitate skill in the areas of decision-making and dimensions of work. While issues in these areas may initially be easy to resolve, with the arrival of children the necessity for mutual respect and accommodation may be even more critical. Lynn Scoresby suggests that what the effective family needs is a couple who are learning to handle these matters so that their family members perceive them as caring for each other and as a unified management team supporting and reinforcing each other's interchanges with family members.

Scoresby also alludes to a third skill that is essential for the successful evolution of a family. In spite of differences there is an evolving unity that emerges through reciprocal caring and keeping the amenities of courtship alive and well. The process of give and take in the early weeks, months, and years of a marriage/relationship could be described as a bonding. The process that keeps the couple together as a successful management team requires caring for each other and saying it and showing it frequently. There will be differences, but the differences are not to be seen as threatening to the basic strength that is their deep caring. This caring is apparent despite harsh words. Ideally, throughout the history of a marriage/relationship and a family, courtship continues unabated. It is our belief that it is when the pressures and stresses of daily living in a family and in the world outside a family displace courtship that nerves wear thin and tempers flare with greater frequency.

For the family with children there is a need to be aware that there is a difference in the relationship between parents and children and the relationship between parents. While we may have an awareness of this difference, however, children often do not. For example, children who have experienced the divorce of their parents may ask, "Will Mommy and Daddy divorce me too?" Upon hearing this question, parents are often dumbfounded that the children are not aware of the difference in these relationships. In a sense, the difference is that no matter what, parents and children are stuck with each other, while spouses/partners are not. Thus the parent–child relationship can be taken for granted (although we do not recommend this), but the spouse/partner relationship cannot. The latter must be constantly affirmed and nurtured through behaviors that mean deep caring. This same deep caring is important in all relationships in the family, but its presence in the marriage/parental relationship is critical.

Each spouse/partner should feel the love and encouragement of individual activities and leisure. The foundation for a successful family is a successfully nurtured relationship between the spouses/partners. The foundation for a successful relationship is adequate, successful individuals. The nurturing of individuality and the marriage/relationship makes it possible to view conflict as an inevitable and normal function of difference and not as a threat to the existence of the marriage/relationship.

The team spirit built on a strong marriage/relationship partnership hopefully will culminate in a strong parental coalition. If the parents satisfy and value one another, the confidence and security, as well as the modeling of appropriate family values, will foster in the children effective communication and a strong sense of identity as males and females.

The concept of a parental coalition also implies that the parents are in reasonable agreement about expectations for their children. Their parenting styles may differ (indeed, perhaps they should differ), but each can live with (not necessarily like) the difference. Dad may pressure more and demand immediate conformity. Mom may coax, encourage, support, and praise more readily. Dad may be quick to criticize and praise more reluctantly. They may each become impatient and upset with the basic way the other parents, but they allow each to do it in his/her own way. This mutually supportive relationship provides a perspective on different and perhaps more creative ways to handle conflict. And in the security of the marital/relationship coalition, parents are able to form a united front when enforcing unpopular, yet necessary, decisions with children and thus are able to maintain family rules and values.

Ideally, both parents can nurture and enforce rules, avoiding the stereotypical father as "heavy" and mother as "softie." Both can be feared and respected enforcers and warm, supportive encouragers and sympathizers. The disagreements that are inevitable in dealing with children can be good opportunities to model mutual respect and effective problem-solving.

Building a successful parental coalition also requires a high level of information exchange and precise, explicit clarification as to what will happen, by whom, and when. Moreover, both are able to back off and discuss how they are communicating and problem-solving. They recognize that their ideas of the way it should be are not necessarily the way it should be. They recognize that they are not independent agents and that whatever they do affects the whole family.

The importance of the marriage/relationship and parental coalition cannot be overemphasized and creating it is a primary task and challenge. The success or failure of this basic enterprise reverberates throughout the whole family for all its years and into the next generation of families. The caring and mutual respect of each spouse for the other provides security and a sense of well-being for the children. In addition, it is from their parents' relationship that children learn to care for and respect others. As children watch parents communicate, make decisions, disagree, and work for resolution of their honest differences, they learn negotiation and decision-making without explicit instruction.

With a strong marriage/relationship and parental coalition each spouse/partner feels freer to try more creative solutions to problems. Security in a relationship fosters more adventuresome and risk-taking behavior. Each spouse/partner is secure in the knowledge that even if the other disagrees, he or she will be supported and differences will be negotiated. Both parents also can be freer to be both warm and strong without vesting each of these characteristics in only one or the other parent.

The strong marriage/relationship and parental coalition serve to maintain an appropriate balance between the importance of the world outside the family and the world within the family. If father works outside the family and mother works exclusively in the family, each may ascribe more relative importance to his or her world. The strong coalition can help give this "taking too seriously" of one's particular world a larger perspective that includes the total life of the family.

The strong marriage/relationship coalition provides a model for the children regarding basic gender role education as they see masculinity and femininity modeled in a particular way. How each spouse is with the other affirms the value each child will place on his or her own identity as male or female. Moreover, children will tend to seek spouses/partners who afford them the same respect and nurturance they have for themselves.

In a strong marriage/relationship coalition, each partner supports and buttresses the other reciprocally and appropriately—when requested. Such a coalition is one in which both partners respect the ability of each to meet challenges without rescuing and thus communicating "you are inadequate."

A measure of the successful marriage/relationship and parental coalition is the relative balance of positive and negative responses. Positive responses should far outweigh the negative. Some research results suggest a nine-to-one ratio is important. Unfortunately, in many marriages/relationships and families people tend to be error-activated. This means that they say nothing until something has gone wrong. An important challenge is to catch spouses/partners and children doing things well. It is the positive comments and surprises that energize and enable us to handle the necessary, mundane tasks that are a large part of the business of the family. This requires conscious attention, but it is well worth the effort as it renews and strengthens both the marriage/relationship and parental coalitions.

We have said a lot in these last few pages, so it seems appropriate to list our ideas about what is important in the successful marriage/relationship and family:

1. Two adequate people, neither of whom needs the other, but who together are more than they were/are separately.

2. A strong, caring, nurturing marriage/relationship coalition.

3. A high level of information exchange and the ability to negotiate and renegotiate to evolve a stable, consistent, yet flexible pattern that is able to change as the family circumstances change.

4. A respect for individuality and differentness and a recognition that the new family will not be a duplicate of either family of origin. The strengths and resources of each are built upon and evolve into feelings of "our family," "our rules," and "our values."

5. With the coming of children this respect for individuality and differentness and the security of the marriage/relationship evolves into a strong parental coalition. Basic expectations of the children are clear, negotiated, and up-front. Differences are worked through to mutual satisfaction. It is through such processes that the childrens' sense of security and well-being is enhanced.

There is an old saying that "Home is a place that when you go there, they have to take you in." We would like to change this to "Home is a place to which you enjoy going, where you are welcomed each and every time you enter, and where you can feel loved, supported, and energized." In this home you may feel a bit paranoid as you "suspect people of plotting to make you happy."

Postscript

In the Introduction to this collection of essays we suggested that you dismiss that which either does not fit one of you or does not fit your relationship. We close with a similar message from a slightly different perspective.

COLLEGE EDUCATION IS NOT FOR INDIANS

In 1774, the Virginia Colony invited six Indian nations (the Iroquois Confederacy) to send six of their young braves to be educated at Williamsburg College. They politely declined as follows:

Greetings:

We know that you highly esteem the kind of learning taught in Colleges, and that the Maintenance of our young Men, while with you, would be very expensive to you. We are convinced, therefore, that you mean to do us Good by your Proposal, and we thank you heartily. But you who are wise, must know that different Nations have different Conceptions of things, and you will therefore not take it amiss, if our Ideas of this kind of Education happen not to be the same with yours. We have had some Experience of it. Several of our Young People were formerly brought up at the colleges of the Northern Provinces; they were instructed in all your sciences; but, when they came back to us, they were bad Runners, ignorant of every means of living in the Woods, unable to bear either Cold or Hunger, knew neither how to build a Cabin, take a Deer, or kill an enemy, spoke our Language imperfectly, were therefore neither fit for Hunters, Warriors, nor Counsellors, they were totally good for nothing. We are, however, not the less obliged by your kind offer, tho we decline accepting it; and to show our grateful Sense of it, if the Gentlemen of Virginia will send us a Dozen of their Sons, we will take care of their Education; instruct them in all we know, and make Men of them.

The Six Indian Nations

Bibliography

Baker, R. (1984). Grouch. *New York Times Magazine*, Feb. 14, Section 6, p. 22.

Brand, S. (1974). *II Cybernetic frontiers*. New York: Random House

Fulgham, R. (1988). *All I really need to know I learned in kindergarten*. New York: Ballantine.

Gibran, K. (1951). *The prophet*. New York: Alfred A. Knopf.

Minuchin, S. (1984). *Family kaleidoscope*. Cambridge, MA: Harvard University Press.

Scoresby, A. (1977). *The marriage dialogue*. Reading, MA: Addison-Wesley.

Watzlawick, P., Weakland, J., & Fisch, R. (1974). *Change: Principles of problem formation and problem resolution*. New York: W.W. Norton.